# Instant Pot Vegan Cookbook

*Healthy Vegan Recipes for Every Taste!*

© Copyright 2016 Gabriel Montana - All rights reserved.

This document is geared towards providing exact and reliable information in regards to the topic and issue covered. The publication is sold with the idea that the publisher is not required to render accounting, officially permitted, or otherwise, qualified services. If advice is necessary, legal or professional, a practiced individual in the profession should be ordered.

- From a Declaration of Principles which was accepted and approved equally by a Committee of the American Bar Association and a Committee of Publishers and Associations.

In no way is it legal to reproduce, duplicate, or transmit any part of this document in either electronic means or in printed format. Recording of this publication is strictly prohibited and any storage of this document is not allowed unless with written permission from the publisher. All rights reserved.

The information provided herein is stated to be truthful and consistent, in that any liability, in terms of inattention or otherwise, by any usage or abuse of any policies, processes, or directions contained within is the solitary and utter responsibility of the recipient reader. Under no circumstances will any legal responsibility or blame be held against the publisher for any reparation, damages, or monetary loss due to the information herein, either directly or indirectly.

Respective authors own all copyrights not held by the publisher.

The information herein is offered for informational purposes solely, and is universal as so. The presentation of the information is without contract or any type of guarantee assurance.

The trademarks that are used are without any consent, and the publication of the trademark is without permission or backing by the trademark owner. All trademarks and brands within this book are for clarifying purposes only and are the owned by the owners themselves, not affiliated with this document.

# Table of Contents

Introduction ............................................................................. 1

Chapter One: Breakfast ............................................................. 4

Chapter Two: Appetizers .......................................................... 8

Chapter Three: Sides ............................................................... 13

Chapter Four: Dishes ............................................................... 29

Chapter Five: Soups ................................................................. 46

Chapter Six: Dessert ................................................................ 59

Conclusion ............................................................................... 65

# Introduction

Are you the owner of an Instant Pot? Are you crazy about the conventional cooking methods it provides and all the creative outlets it offers? Are you dying to explore what you can do with your pot from the get-go? Do you try to live a health-conscious lifestyle by eating vegan-based foods? Download your cookbook today and discover the many recipes that you can use with your Instant Pot.

This cookbook includes recipes of all sorts:

- Appetizers
- Breakfast
- Sides
- Dishes
- Soups
- Desserts
- And many ways that you can make these recipes your own and fit them to your own desired tastes.

Take the time to learn what you are capable of with your Instant Pot today! If you are ready to put your new best kitchen accessory to work, learn the many ways you can create savory meals and treats for your friends and family. Discover the tasty side of a vegan-friendly diet that your body and taste buds will thank you for. Make use of your new best friend in the kitchen today and learn how to cook healthy meals in a fast, clean, and fun way. Find ways to make great use of the accessories included with your Instant Pot.

Owning an Instant Pot gives you endless meal possibilities and ideas to incorporate into any craving you might have. Explore your talents with your conventional helper in the kitchen by cutting your cooking times in half or even less, using less energy for your electric bill and yourself.

The Instant Pot is a pressure cooker that provides a convenient form of cooking. It is programmable and can speed up the cooking time to be 2-6 times faster than it would be using other methods. It uses up to 70% less energy as well. Your Instant Pot can serve as a slow cooker, pressure cooker, rice cooker, steamer, saute pan, and a warmer. There are plenty of ways to incorporate your instant pot with your cooking methods, daily life, or any social event such as potlucks, for example.

Some of the positives that come with the Instant Pot make it a health conscious accessory for anyone that is busy but also trying to live a healthier, more convenient lifestyle. Your Instant Pot will preserve the nutrition in the cooked ingredients and is less likely to cook the vitamins and nutrients out of any vegetable, fruit, or grain cooked in your instant pot. This also provides a cleaner cooking experience, thus making it more convenient. The accessories provided with your instant pot can be very useful when discovering the many ways you can cook different ingredients in your instant pot. Make great use of these accessories in order to easily cook your meal of choice.

For those on the run and living a busy lifestyle, you can plan your meals ahead of time and have your instant pot cook your dinner for you while you are away at work. Arrive home with little preparation to do in order to have a warm, healthy and delicious meal. Easily do meal-planning and preparation with different recipes and your instant pot. Most recipes can be easily stored afterward either as great leftovers or convenient meals throughout the week to save you time, energy, and help you avoid going through the drive thru.

If you are the lucky owner of an Instant Pot, you will need to get started off with some great recipes to use in your convenient kitchen appliance. Included in the recipe book are a variety of recipes that will fit anyone's preference. Regardless of why you choose vegan meals over other meal types, they cannot be argued unhealthy. There are many benefits to come from this type of lifestyle diet. Just because you are cutting some ingredients out of your lifestyle doesn't mean that your food has to be boring and tasteless. There are plenty of ingredients that you can incorporate into any vegan meal and the instant pot is a great choice for cooking your vegan ingredients.

Prepare your Instant Pot and your taste buds for some incredible food coming your way. Discover all the types of delicious and healthy foods that can be prepared right inside your Instant Pot and your home. The recipes included in this book will give you plenty of creative ideas of the endless possibilities that you can use your Instant Pot for. The recipes can be added to and adjusted in order to fit your taste and cravings.

Once you get used working your instant pot, you will start making up your own recipes in time. The instant pot will only provide a great cooking experience that will give you the ability to experiment with your food and planned meals. There is plenty that you can do with your kitchen accessory and number one helper. Make your instant pot your best friend in the kitchen and explore all the ways that you can cook great meals that taste amazing, are cooked quick and great, and become your own with your touch of desired tastes.

# Chapter One: Breakfast

If you are looking for delicious alternatives to regular toast and jam, or a bowl of cereal
with soy milk, here are a couple of ideas you can use to start your day off right with great sources of protein to give you adequate amounts of energy to get you to lunch, whenever that may be for you.

## Wheat and Vegetable Breakfast

Wheat berries are larger kernels of grain. These can be incorporated into plenty of recipes. It is considered a type of fruit but it can be similar to oatmeal in ways. This recipe can be a great alternative to quiche. You could make this dish for all meals of the day. You could plan for breakfast and then save the leftovers for other meals if you get too busy to cook any more food the rest of the day. This dish is very convenient but requires some extra preparation. After you have prepared the dish, you can easily refrigerate it and save for later.

This recipe will serve 4 to 5 people.

Prepping time: 15 minutes
Cooking time: 30 minutes
Total time: 45 minutes

Calories per serving: 213.20

What to include:

6 1/2 cups water
2 cups of white wheat berries
2 medium potatoes either cut sliced or cubed
2 medium onions either cut sliced or cubed
2 cups of sliced carrots
5 stalks of celery that are sliced
2 to 4 smashed garlic cloves (this is optional)
1 tablespoon of either oil or vegan butter
1 tablespoon of salt
1 teaspoon of poultry seasoning
1/8 teaspoon of thyme

What to do:

1. You have to allow your wheat berries to soak in water overnight in your instant pot.
2. Use a separate frying pan to saute the onions, celery, and the garlic (if using any), with around 2 to 3 teaspoons of an oil of your choice or vegan butter.
3. You will then use the "multi-grain" setting provided on your instant pot and cook the wheat berries, potatoes, and the carrots.
4. After the wheat berries are done and fully cooked, you will then add your sautéed vegetables.
5. You can then let your dish simmer using your instant pot as a slow cooker. The dish can simmer for about 30 minutes to let the flavors mingle, or you can instantly serve the dish warm.

# Peaches and "Cream" Oatmeal

When you don't have much time to prepare for a meal, this is a more convenient alternative. It is a simple mix and cook meal that can prepare fresh in the morning. You could add a little bit of vanilla extract starting out with ¼ of a teaspoon of extract to add a little bit of flavor to your breakfast. Add your own desired amount of sweetener, whether that be agave, brown sugar, or whatever sweetener alternative. If you are more of a strawberry, raspberry, or blueberry person, you could substitute the peaches for your own desired amount of fruit of your choice. You could mix and match different fruits as well. Have fun with the flavors and make the recipe your own.

This recipe will serve about 3 people. The recipe can be easily doubled as well.

Calories per serving: 187

Prepping time: 5 minutes
Cooking time: 10 minutes
Total time: 15 minutes

What to include:

1 cup of oats
1 cup of coconut milk, or any vegan milk substitute
2 cups of water
2 peaches that are diced

What to do:

1. You will mix all of the ingredients in a separate bowl and then add your mixture into your instant pot.
2. Set "Manual" and then "Adjust" to 3.
3. Your mixture will cook for 10 minutes and then you will use the natural pressure release.
4. Sweeten as desired and then serve.

# Chapter Two: Appetizers

Appetizers can make great snacks and accompany you while entertaining guests or enjoying a few friends over. Here are a couple of appetizers that can be used to impress and introduce your guests to new food items that they will fall in love with as soon as they taste. You and your instant pot will get to take the credit for all the great flavor.

## Chickpea Hummus

Make your own chickpea hummus dip at home. Dip with pita bread, chips, or crackers of your choice. Hummus makes a great snack full of healthy protein to keep you going through your day. With plenty of herbs added in the recipe, this dip is full of flavor that will leave your taste buds satisfied.

This recipe will serve around 6 to 8 people.

Prepping time: 5 minutes
Cooking time: 25 minutes
Total time: 30 minutes

Serving Size: 1/8th of the batch.
Calories per serving: 109

What to include:

6 cups of water
1 cup of dry chickpeas that are either soaked or quick-soaked
3 to 4 garlic cloves

1 bay leaf
1 juiced lemon
2 rounded tablespoons of tahini
½ teaspoon of sea salt
½ bunch of parsley (chopped will be about ¼ cup)
¼ teaspoon of powdered cumin
paprika extract
extra virgin olive oil

What to do:

1. You will rinse off the chickpeas after soaking them and then place them inside your instant pot.
2. Add your 6 cups of water into the instant pot along with 2 crushed garlic cloves and the bay leaf.
3. You will then close the lid of your instant pot and lock it. Then, cook for 18 minutes at high pressure.
4. Use the natural release to open the instant pot lid after the cooking time is done. Allow it to cool down for up to 10 minutes.
5. You will then drain the chickpeas and save the cooking liquid in a separate container. You will need the cooking liquid to add to the chickpeas during the pureeing process. You can save some chickpeas for a fancy garnish touch at the end. But this is only optional. Pull out the bay leaf and then allow the chickpeas to cool.
6. Next, you will puree the chickpeas after they have had time to cool down. You can do this using a food processor, stick blender, or a potato masher.
7. Add ½ cup of the cooking liquid that was saved after the draining process. Then, add the tahini, the lemon juice, cumin spice, and either 1 or 2 garlic cloves depending on what you prefer.

8. Puree your ingredients in order to mix everything well and to get a creamy consistency. When your hummus mixture has desired consistency to your preference, add salt and mix well.

9. Place your hummus mixture in a serving bowl or on a plate in a mound. Make a crater in the middle of the mound and then pour in olive oil and sprinkle paprika, parsley and your saved whole chickpeas for the fancy garnishing touch.

# Eggplant and Olive Spread

You can use this spread to go with any bread or crackers of your choice. The mix is very flexible and savory with plenty of olive oil and herbs. This adds plenty of fiber and protein to your daily diet, along with plenty of flavors as well.

This recipe will serve 4 to 6 people.

Prepping time: 5 minutes
Cooking time: 18 minutes
Total time: 23 minutes

Serving Size: 1/6th of the batch
Calories per serving: 155.5

What to include:

2 pounds of eggplant
1 cup of water
3 to 4 cloves of garlic
4 tablespoons of olive oil
1 juiced lemon or about ¼ cup of lemon juice
4 tablespoons of olive oil
1 tablespoon of tahini
1 teaspoon of salt
¼ cup of black olives that are pitted
thyme
extra virgin olive oil

What to do:

1. To start off, peel your eggplant with alternating stripes of skin and no skin. Then, slice into big chunks and use the larger chunks in order to cover up the bottom of your instant pot. The rest of your remaining eggplant can be roughly chopped.

2. Pre-heat your instant pot to medium heat and then add the olive oil keeping the lid off. Once the oil is heated, place your larger chunks of eggplant to cover up the bottom of your instant pot. You want to fry and caramelize these pieces for about 5 minutes. Throw in the garlic cloves with the skin still on them.

3. Flip the large pieces of eggplant and then add in the remaining chunks of eggplant that were roughly chopped. Add in salt and water. Then, close the lid of your instant pot and lock it.

4. Cook for 3 minutes at high pressure. After the cooking time is done, you will release the pressure through the valve. You can remove most of the brown liquid by placing your instant pot in the base of your sink and tipping it on its side.

5. Remove the garlic cloves that were added in and any of their skins that might have come off during the cooking process.

6. Add the tahini, the lemon juice, cooked and uncooked garlic cloves along with the black olives. By using a stick blender or a food processor, you can puree all the ingredients together. You can tilt your instant pot sideways in order to move everything into the nook and easily mix everything in that position.

7. Pour your finished mixture into a serving dish and then sprinkle thyme on top. You can add any leftover black olives and olive oil for a fancy garnishing touch.

# Chapter Three: Sides

Sides can make a great addition to any dish that you are cooking for your main course.
They can bring out the flavors of your main dish when paired well. Listed in this chapter of the book are some sides that can easily be incorporated into any meal. These sides are healthier alternatives that what the "non-vegan" version would be. Add any ingredients or seasoning to fit your desired tastes.

## Steamed Artichokes

These steamed artichokes will top off any dish or meal of your choice. Serve them as a snack, appetizer, or side. Add or ignore any ingredients that you don't care for in order to dress the artichokes to your desired preference. Steam the artichokes with your desired toppings or no toppings at all and eat them with only vegan butter and salt.

This recipe will serve about 4 people.

Prepping time: 5 minutes
Cooking time: 20 minutes
Total time: 25 minutes

Serving size: ½ artichoke
Calories per serving: 77.5

What to include:

2 medium artichokes(or various sizes. Refer to steam instructions for different sizes of artichokes.)
1 cup of water
1 lemon that is sliced in half
2 tablespoons of vegan mayonnaise
1 teaspoon of Dijon mustard
1 pinch of paprika

Steam the small artichokes for 5 minutes, medium sized for 10 minutes, and larger ones for 15.

What to do:

1. You should properly trim your artichokes. Cut off any edges that are spiny by using kitchen shears. You want to trim and spines of surrounding leaves. You want to remove any damaged outer leaves and then wash off your artichokes well. Use your lemon slices to wipe any cut edges in order to keep them from oxidizing.
Slice the bottom of the artichoke to give it a flat surface to rest on for the cooking process.
2. Add the water to your instant pot. Then, add the artichokes and place any stem pieces in the steamer basket and then lower inside the instant pot. You will want to place your artichokes facing upwards and then spritz any leftover juice that remains in your lemon slices.
3. Close and lock the lid of your instant pot. At high pressure, cook for 10 minutes.
4. Use the natural release method after the cooking time is done.
5. After the time is up, you can check the doneness of your artichokes by doing a quick taste test and removing one of the leaves. If you think your artichokes are not soft enough and need

more time to cook, cook for a few more minutes and then use the normal release method when the cooking time is up.

6. Once your artichokes are done, mix the vegan mayonnaise with the Dijon mustard and then place in a small container that can be used for dipping. Sprinkle the mixture with paprika and serve your artichokes warm.

# Italian Style Potato Salad

For a different and healthier potato salad choice, try out this recipe. No mayonnaise or egg additives make it a great alternative. Olive oil and white wine vinegar are used to coat and add flavor along with onion, parsley, and regular salt and pepper. This potato salad recipe alternative has plenty of flavor with a lot fewer calories and no dairy or egg products involved in the making.

This recipe will serve 6 to 8 people.

Prepping time: 5 minutes
Cooking time: 15 minutes
Total time: 20 minutes

Serving size: ⅛th
Calories per serving: 237.6

What to include:

  3 pounds of red or regular potatoes that are largely diced
  ¼ medium onion or ½ of z medium red onion that is finely chopped
  1 ½ cups of water
  1 bunch of parsley that is finely chopped and includes stems and leaves
  4 to 5 tablespoons of extra virgin olive oil
  3 to 4 tablespoons of white wine vinegar
  1 teaspoon salt
  a dash of ground black pepper

What to do:

1. First, set up your instant pot with the water and the trivet accessory.
2. Scrub and wash off your potatoes well in warm water. Then, cut them in one inch cubes and place them in the trivet steamer basket.
3. Close and lock the lid of your instant pot. You will then cook it for 5 minutes at high pressure.

While the potatoes are cooking, you want to start chopping up the onion and then set aside in a small bowl with the vinegar, salt, and pepper included. Go ahead and finely chop up the parsley and include the stems and leaves.

4. Use the normal release method in order to release the pressure after the cooking time is done.
5. Place the potatoes in a bowl with the onions and then pour the olive oil and mix in the vinegar and onions. Let the potatoes cool down. Ten minutes should be plenty of time for the cooling process.
6. After the potatoes have cooled down to at least room temperature, add the parsley and then serve either immediately or you can let it chill overnight in the refrigerator.

# Corn on the Cob

Experience a better cooking when cooking your ears of corn. The corn will cook more thoroughly and evenly, not to mention it is a much quicker alternative. Add your own amount of vegan butter and salt, or olive oil as an alternative.

This recipe will provide 8 servings or ears of corn.

Serving size: 2 ears
Calories per serving: 63

What to include:

2 cups of water
8 ears of corn (or less if you don't need this much)

What to do:

1. Cut off the stubs of the ears of corn and remove the husks if any are still attached.
2. Add your water to the instant pot and then place the ears of corn vertically making sure to keep the larger ends in the water and the top and smaller ends pointed upward. For the taller ears of corn, you can either place them diagonally or cut them in half. You want to make sure that you leave space around each ear of corn in order to allow the steam to evenly cook each ear and the kernels.
3. Close and lock the lid of your instant pot. You will then cook for 2 minutes at high pressure.
4. After the cooking time is done, use the normal release method.
5. Serve with your preference of salt and your choice of vegan butter.

# Cranberry Sauce

Make your own cranberry sauce at home. This makes a great addition to the traditional Thanksgiving meal without too much time to prepare and cook. You can keep your spare dried cranberries around as a snack, salad topping, and a backup for delicious cranberry sauce. By re-hydrating the cranberries and some of their own juices, you will have a great sauce you can use for your own dipping desires or to eat it as it is.

This recipe will provide 1 cup of cranberry sauce. Each serving is 3 teaspoons worth.

Prepping time: 1 minute
Cooking time: 14 minutes
Total time: 15 minutes

Serving size: 3 teaspoons
Calories per serving: 30.1

What to include:

1 ½ cup of water
1 cup of dried cranberries
¾ cup of cranberry juice cocktail
1 teaspoon of lemon juice

What to do:

1. To start off, add all of the ingredients into your instant pot. Close and lock the lid and then cook at high heat for 3 minutes.
2. Release the pressure manually by letting out the pressure from the valve in short bursts. Wait ten seconds before releasing any

more pressure if by chance anything more than just steam is releasing from the valve.

3. To puree the ingredients together, you can use a food processor or a stick blender in order to do so. If using a stick blender, you can tilt your instant pot sideways to allow the ingredients to gather in a nook and adequately mix everything together. You want to keep in mind that you are not trying to liquefy the ingredients. You want a sauce consistency.

4. After you puree the ingredients, you want to let the mixture simmer in your instant pot without a lid. Make sure to stir frequently until you have reached the desired thickness of your preference. This process can take around 5 minutes. Once you are able to drag your utensil across the bottom of the instant pot and see the base, you can turn the heat off and let the mixture set uncovered for around 10 minutes.

5. You can either serve your sauce warm and fresh or refrigerate it for up to a week to allow it to be firmer.

# Cumin Millet

Millet is similar to Quinoa but can be considered healthier in some ways. When you want to prepare a healthy side for a Mexican dish, this will fit well with any dish of that sort. This recipe has plenty of herbs and spices in order to add a unique and great taste to the mixture. Use it as a side, or a building block to your own vegan Mexican recipe.

This recipe will serve 4 to 6 people.

Prepping time: 5 minutes
Cooking time: 15 minutes
Total time: 20 minutes

Serving size: ⅛th or about ¾ cup
Calories per serving: 100.8

For millet, the ratio is grain to water at 1: 1.5.
You do not want to fill the cooker over halfway full with the water.

What to include:

2 cups of organic millet
3 cups of water
3 teaspoons of cumin seeds
1 large white onion that is halved and sliced into strips
1 tablespoon of vegetable oil
1 teaspoon of crushed cardamom or about ¼ teaspoon powder, or 3 whole pods
1-inch cinnamon stick
1 bay leaf
1 teaspoon of salt

What to do:

1. On medium heat, pre-heat your instant pot. Then, add the oil, bay leaf, cinnamon stick, the cumin and the cardamom.
2. Saute the ingredients until you can hear the cumin start to crackle.
3. Then, add the onion and continue to saute for about 5 minutes until it softens.
4. Then you want to add the millet and make sure to coat it well with your choice of cooking oil. Then, add the water and salt.
5. Close and lock the lid of your instant pot. You will then cook for one minute at high pressure.
6. Use the natural release to release all of the pressure after the cooking time is done. The pressure will come down on its own after about 10 minutes or so.
7. You can fluff up the millet with a fork or other utensil and then serve.

# "Baked" Potatoes

The conventional way of baking of potatoes in the oven can take 70 to 90 minutes.

Relying on your instant pot will give you "baked" potatoes in 25 minutes. With the high-pressure steaming process, the steam will cook your potatoes evenly and quick regardless of their size.

Each potato is considered one serving.

Calories per serving: about 160

Prepping time: 5-8 minutes
Cooking time: 12-15 minutes
Total time: 17-23 minutes

What to include:

Large russet potatoes, as much as you need
Around 1 cup of water for every 2 potatoes
Olive oil
Salt
Any vegan-friendly topping of your choice

What to do:

1. Use warm water to wash and brush your potatoes. Then, place them in a heat-resistant bowl that is either ceramic or steel.
2. Place your water in the instant pot.
3. Place the bowl of the potatoes on top of the steam rack accessory. Then, you will choose the steam program and allow the potatoes to cook for 12-15 minutes.

4. Use the normal release after the cooking time is done and remove the potatoes.

5. You can poke holes in your potatoes and then lightly coat them with olive oil but this is only optional. You can also grill you potatoes or place them in a toaster oven for 5 minutes to give them a crispy, baked effect.

# Sweet Potatoes

When you are in the mood for sweet potatoes, take the time to cook them in your instant pot instead of the oven. This will save you lots of time and give you a better tasting experience. Top with brown sugar and a great vegan butter substitute in order to bring out the sweet flavor of the potatoes.

Each large sweet potato is about 165 calories (without toppings).

Prepping time: 10 minutes
Cooking time: 15 minutes
Total time: 25 minutes

What to include:

2 to 3 large sweet potatoes
½ cup of water
extra virgin olive oil

What to do:

1. First, you want to scrub your potatoes with warm water and then lightly coat them with the extra virgin olive oil and then wrap them up in aluminum foil.
2. Then, pour the water into the instant pot. Then, add the trivet accessory and place the sweet potatoes on top of the trivet.
3. You will then close the lid of the instant pot and lock it. Push the steam button and allow them to cook for 15 minutes.

4. After the cooking time is done, you will use the normal release method in order to release all of the pressure. Remove the sweet potatoes and remove the aluminum foil from them once they have cooled down and serve immediately.

# Wheat Berry Salad

This makes a great salad that you can easily store in the refrigerator. This is a great recipe to use for meal planning. Set aside portioned amounts in your refrigerator and easily take with you to work or wherever your busy schedule may take you. This way you will save time, money, and have a healthier eating experience as a result. This is best served chilled but it isn't necessary. If you have been a fan of chicken salad, this can be a great alternative. Use the mixture as a substitute to make sandwiches or eat it by itself.

This recipe will serve 3 to 4 people.

Calories per serving: about 270

Prepping time: 4 hours and 10 minutes
Cooking time: 15-20 minutes
Total time: 4 hours and 25-30 minutes

What to include:

1 cup of wheat berries
2 cups of water
¼ cup of raspberry vinegar (you can make your own by soaking raspberries in vinegar)
¾ cup of dried blueberries
¾ cup of thinly sliced green onions
½ cup of dried apricots
½ cup of toasted and chopped almonds
3 tablespoons of vegetable oil
2 tablespoons of chopped parsley
1 tablespoon of balsamic vinegar

2 teaspoons of Dijon mustard
¾ teaspoon of salt
½ teaspoon pepper

What to do:

1. First, you want to rinse your wheat berries with cold water and place them in a bowl filled with cold water and allow them to soak overnight beforehand and then drain them in the morning.
2. Place the wheat berries in your instant pot with the water. You will then cook at high pressure for 15 to 20 minutes. Then, you will use the normal release method to release the pressure once the cooking time is done. Rinse them in cold water afterward.
3. With a whisk, mix together the raspberry vinegar, the balsamic vinegar, Dijon mustard, the salt and pepper in a bowl. You will then gradually mix all the ingredients together until everything is well blended.
4. Then, you want to stir in the onions, blueberries, apricots, parsley, and the almonds.
5. Let the mixture sit for 30 minutes and then stir in the wheat berries.
6. Cover and chill your salad in the refrigerator for at least 4 hours and up to 24 hours. The chilling process will allow all of the flavors to mingle.

# Chapter Four: Dishes

There are plenty of dishes that can be made with your instant pot. In this chapter of the book you will find recipes for every type of food with unique twists that make every taste interesting and healthy all at the same time. Add or ignore any added ingredients that don't fit your taste. Feel free to play around with flavors, herbs, and spices.

## Chickpea Curry with Brown Rice

If you have a smaller pressure cooker, the quantities can be halved and you can use a smaller heat dish to cook the rice. If you are doubling this recipe, do not exceed the pressure cooker's capacity by half with the chickpeas cooking. This is a great meal but takes a little bit of time to cook but is worth the wait. This is a great dish to cook when you are in the mood to cook and enjoy some time in the kitchen.

This recipe will serve 4 to 5 people

Calories per serving: about 265.75

Prepping time: 10 minutes
Cooking time: 26-28 minutes
Total time: 36-38 minutes

What to include:

1 ½ cups of brown rice with 2 ¼ cups of water
1 cup of chickpeas with 2 cups of water and either soaked overnight or quick soaked
1 red onion that is chopped
2 tablespoons of chana masala
2 tablespoons of tomato concentrate
1 tablespoon of vegetable oil
1 tablespoon of minced garlic
1 tablespoon of minced ginger
1 teaspoon of salt

What to do:

1. To start out, add the rice and the recommended water into a 4 cup capacity container that is heat proof. The container should have a handle in order to lower and raise it out of your instant pot. Set this container to the side.
2. Pre-heat your instant pot to medium without the lid. Then, you will add the oil and onion in order to saute for about 7 minutes until the onions start to caramelize.
3. Next, add the chana masala, the garlic, and the ginger and continue to saute for about 30 more seconds until the garlic starts to cook.
4. Pour in the water, chickpeas, and the tomato concentrate into your instant pot. Lower steam basket or trivet into the instant pot with the chickpeas.
5. Next, you will lower the uncovered container onto the steamer basket or trivet.
Close and lock the lid of the instant pot. At high pressure, cook for 18-20 minutes.

6. You will then open the instant pot by using the natural pressure release method after the cooking time is done. The pressure should come down on its own for about 10 minutes. Manually release any remaining pressure after 10 minutes.

7. Lift the container out of the instant pot very carefully and then fluff the rice and serve immediately on dishes.

# Lentils in Tomato sauce

When you are craving pasta but you don't want the noodles and instead would like something packed with nutrients, this recipe will give you a great fix. Each serving can provide a recommended daily value of 22% Folate, 12.3% manganese, and 9% iron. Something good to think about when cooking and enjoying. This can also make a good recipe to do some meal planning with. This gives you plenty of servings to last all week if you are cooking for yourself. Either way, you have plenty to work with, and fewer calories to deal with but plenty of protein to keep you going.

This recipe will serve about 6 people.

Serving size: One-sixth
Calories per serving: 104.8

What to include:

1 medium onion that is chopped
1 ½ cups of chopped tomatoes
1 ½ cups of dry lentils
2 cups of water
1 stalk of celery that is chopped using all the stems and leaves
1 medium green pepper
1 tablespoon of extra virgin olive oil
1 teaspoon of curry powder (this is optional) salt and pepper to taste

What to do:

1. You will pre-heat your instant pot and then add olive oil, onion, celery, and pepper. Saute until the onion starts to soften.
2. After the mix has softened, add the tomatoes and mix well. Sprinkle any salt, pepper, and curry if you are using any.
3. Next, add the lentils and the water. Mix well and make sure to rub the base of the instant pot to get any bits that may have stuck during the saute process.
4. Close and lock the lid of the instant pot and then cook for 15 minutes at high pressure.
5. You will use the natural release method in order to release the pressure after the cooking time is done. You want to wait for the pressure to come down on its own. This should take about 10 minutes. After 10 minutes, release any remaining pressure manually through the valve.
6. Open your instant pot and remove, then serve immediately.

# Zucchini Pesto Pasta Sauce

For times that you want a healthier pasta sauce, and something a bit different, Zucchini
Pesto Pasta sauce will do the trick. This is a great alternative compared to regular tomato paste-like sauce. This can be placed over pasta or anything that you decide to substitute noodles for. It will create a nice green mixture packed full of nutrients. This sauce will provide 29% recommended daily values of Vitamin A, 15% of manganese and 13% of Vitamin C for each serving.

This recipe will serve 4 to 6 people.

Yields enough sauce for 16oz pasta package.

Prepping time: 3 minutes
Cooking time: 10 minutes
Total time: 13 minutes

Serving size: 1 portion
Calories per serving: 71.4

What to include:

1 ½ pounds of zucchini that is roughly chopped
1 onion that is roughly chopped
2 cloves of garlic that is roughly chopped and minced
¾ cup of water
1 tablespoon of olive oil
1 bunch of basil with the leaves picked off
1 tablespoon of extra virgin olive oil
1 ½ teaspoon of salt

What to do:

1. Pre-heat your instant pot to medium heat and then add the oil and onion in order to saute for about 4 minutes until it starts to soften.
2. Add the zucchini, salt, and the water. Close and lock the lid of your instant pot. At high pressure, cook for 3 minutes.
3. After the cooking time is done, use the normal release method.
4. Toss in the garlic and the basil leaves. Then, use an immersion blender in order to puree the ingredients until all the garlic and basil is mixed well.
5. Mix your sauce with your choice of pasta and then serve with an extra amount of virgin olive oil as desired.

# Santa Fe Style Enchiladas Verdes

For great enchiladas without chicken, beef, or dairy, this recipe will fill your enchilada craving. Just substitute any dairy products you would regularly use with a great vegan alternative. Find vegan cheese or vegan sour cream. Added pico de gallo will make a great topping as well. Freshly made guacamole and chips will pair well with this amazing dish. Use as many corn tortillas as desired or needed for your preference. It takes a little more time to cook but this recipe is well worth the preparation and cooking time.

This recipe will serve 4 to 5 people.

Calories per serving: about 240

Prepping time: 15 minutes
Cooking time: 36-42 minutes
Total time: 51-57 minutes

What to include:

10 tomatillos
3 poblano peppers
2 zucchinis that are thinly sliced
¼ cup of white onion that is finely minced
1 cup of corn
¼ cup of cilantro
1 cup of shredded vegan jack cheese
a handful of mushrooms that are thinly sliced
corn tortillas
1 teaspoon of salt

What to do:

1. To get started, place the peppers on a cooking sheet and then place in oven. Make sure to space them 3 inches apart from each other. Cook in the oven for 10-12 minutes at 350 degrees. Make sure to turn with tongs and then cook for another 8-10 minutes until they are charred.
2. After the peppers have cooked, remove them and set aside in a plastic bag and then steam for 10 minutes in order to remove the skins. It is okay if you can't get all of the skins off. Make sure to take off the stem and remove the seeds.
3. Husk the tomatillos and wash them off in warm water in order to remove any sticky film on them. Pat them dry and then place them on the cooking sheet you just used. Cook them for 10-12 minutes until they are browned. Then, remove and set aside.
4. Use a food processor or a blender in order to make a salsa mixture. Combine your tomatillos, cilantro, salt, and poblano peppers in a mixer of your choice and pulse until you get a smooth mixture. Save this for the layering of the enchiladas. This is your salsa verde mixture.
5. In the bottom of your instant pot, spread the mixture and then layer the tortillas.
Then, layer the zucchini, mushrooms, and the chopped poblano peppers.
Sprinkle the shredded vegan jack cheese and drizzle any remaining salsa verde mixture that is left over.
6. Place your trivet in the bottom of your instant pot and then add 1 cup of water.
You will then close the lid of the instant pot and lock it. Cook for 8 minutes at high pressure and then use the normal release method in order to release the pressure after the cooking time is done. Remove the dish and let it cool. Serve afterwards.

# Asparagus Spring Risotto

When you need a light and nutritious dish, this recipe will be the right fix for you if you have enough time to prepare and cook a delicious and nutritious meal. You can use whatever asparagus of your choice for this recipe, though you might want to choose thicker asparagus pieces that will hold up better in your instant pot. The asparagus mixed with plenty of flavors and an adequate amount of rice makes it a very healthy and convenient dish to prepare. Feel free to play around with any added flavors.

This recipe will serve 4 people.

Prepping time: 10 minutes
Cooking time: 30 minutes
Total time: 40 minutes

Serving size: ¼th (about 1½ cups)
Calories per serving: 230

What to include:

1 pound of asparagus
1 medium red onion that is chopped
4 cups of water
2 cups of Arborio rice
¼ cup of dry white wine
1 lemon wedge that is squeezed or about ½ teaspoon of lemon juice
1 tablespoon of olive oil
2 teaspoons of salt
extra virgin olive oil for fancy garnishing

What to do:

1. First, you want to trim up your asparagus by removing the woody stems. Slice your asparagus into small pieces and chop up until the tops. Slice away the tips and then set aside.
2. Then, add your asparagus and water into your instant pot. You will then close the lid of your instant pot and lock it. Cook for 12 minutes at high pressure and use the normal release method in order to release the pressure from your instant pot after the cooking time is done.
3. You will then pour out the asparagus stems and the stock water mixture into a heat-safe measuring cup and then measure out 4 cups with a ¼ cup of extra liquid. This will be your micro-stock.
4. Keeping your instant pot still heated, add the onion and the olive oil Mix the two together until the onions have started to soften.
5. Next, you will add the rice and mix it well with the oils and the onions. The rice will start to become slightly translucent. Keep stirring until the kernels start to turn white again. This process should take only about 2 minutes.
6. Add in the white wine and then stir until all of it has evaporated.
7. Add the asparagus and the micro-stock with the asparagus tips and the salt. Mix the ingredients together and try to prevent any sticking or burning by making sure to scrape the base of the instant pot every now and then.
8. You will then close the lid of the instant pot and lock it. You will cook it for 6 minutes at high pressure. You will use the normal release method in order to release the pressure after the cooking time is done.
9. Add a squeeze of the lemon juice and then mix well. Serve with an extra swirl of extra virgin olive oil for a fancy garnishing touch.

# Lima Bean Casserole

When you need to fix up a quick casserole as a great alternative, this lima bean casserole will give you what you need. It is a simple mix and cook recipe that has little prep time and under 30 minutes of cooking time. Feel free to play around with any flavors that are added and exclude ingredients that you don't particularly care for. It is definitely an interesting recipe that people are more than likely new to if you are bringing it to a social gathering or trying something new for your family.

This recipe will serve 3 to 4 people.

Prepping time: 5 minutes
Cooking time: 24 minutes
Total time: 29 minutes

Calories per serving: 175

What to include:

1 pound of lima beans
1 cup of vegan sour cream
¾ cup of vegan butter
¾ of brown sugar
1 tablespoon of dark Karo syrup
1 tablespoon of dry mustard
2 teaspoons of salt

What to do:

1. You will first want to soak the lima beans in 10 cups of water and add 1 teaspoon worth of salt or so.
2. You will then cook the lima beans in your instant pot for 4 minutes at high pressure. After the cooking time is done, use the "keep warm" setting for about 10 minutes and then use the quick release method in order to release the pressure.
3. You will then want to rinse off and drain the beans and then place them back in the instant pot. Add the rest of the remaining ingredients and mix gently together.
4. Cook the rest of the ingredients for 10 minutes at high pressure. Then use the quick release method again and serve immediately.

# Spaghetti Squash

When you need a good substitute for noodles, spaghetti squash can do the trick. Trading out noodles for healthy ingredients is a great alternative. Spaghetti squash could be paired with the Zucchini Pesto pasta sauce easily instead of regular noodles. This recipe can also be easily stored in your refrigerator and used to portion out and use for meal planning for your upcoming week. Spaghetti squash can chill and even freeze quite well. The difference between regular noodles and spaghetti squash isn't even that obvious at first but the taste has much to offer and there are obvious health benefits to the alternative.

This recipe will serve 4 people.

Prepping time: 10 minutes
Cooking time: 15 minutes
Total time: 30 minutes

Serving size: ¼th
Calories per serving: 88.6

What to include:

1 medium spaghetti squash
3 to 5 cloves of garlic that is sliced
1 small bunch of fresh sage or about ½ cup of fresh sage leaves
1 cup of water
2 tablespoons of olive oil
1 teaspoon of salt
1/8 teaspoon of nutmeg

What to do:

1. Cut your squash in half and then scoop out the seeds.
2. Add the water into the instant pot and lower the squash into it with the halves facing upwards and overlapping them if needed.
3. You will then close the lid of the instant pot and cook for 3 to 4 minutes at high pressure.
4. While the squash is cooking, take a saute pan and add together the garlic, sage, and olive oil. Cook on low heat and occasionally stir the mixture. The sage leaves will end up turning to a dark green color once they start to fry. Make sure not to burn any of the garlic slices.
5. After the cooking time is done, release the pressure using the normal method. Open the lid and take a fork and tease the fibers of the squash. Place the fibers into the saute pan.
6. Once all of the fibers are in the pan, turn off the heat and then sprinkle with salt and nutmeg. Mix all the ingredients together and then serve immediately.

# Kamut, Orange & Arugula Salad

Kamut grains can be similar to wheat berries. They are a type of wheat that has higher levels of protein, amino acids, and vitamin E. This salad is similar to the wheat berry salad recipe except that it contains actual leaves. This can also be easily stored for meal planning. Place in the refrigerator in order to preserve the ingredients. Separate out into portions for the rest of the week. This recipe will give you more portions than the wheat berry salad. You could even experiment and try placing the salad in bread and make into a sandwich.

This recipe will serve 6 to 8 people.

Prepping time: 10 minutes
Cooking time: 30 minutes
Total time: 40 minutes

Serving size: ⅛th
Calories per serving: 126.9

What to include:

1 cup of whole Kamut grains
2 cups of water
2 medium blood oranges that are peeled and sliced in cross-wise segments that are   separated
half of a lemon
½ cup of vegan romano cheese (this is only optional)
1 bunch of rocket arugula
about ½ cup of walnuts that are roughly chopped
1 tablespoon of cold-pressed extra virgin olive oil
1 teaspoon vegetable oil

1 teaspoon salt

What to do:

1. In a large bowl, place the kamut inside with the water and the juice of the half lemon. Soak this overnight or for 12 hours. After it has soaked, rinse and strain the kamut.
2. Add the kamut, water, salt and vegetable oil to the instant pot. You will then close the lid of the instant pot and lock it. Cook for 15 to 18 minutes at high pressure and then use the natural release method in order to release the pressure after the cooking time is done. You can open the lid after the pressure has come down on its own. This should take about 10 minutes. If you are cooking unsoaked kamut, you can cook it at high pressure for 20-30 minutes. For every cup of kamut that you use in your recipe, you should add three cups of water to accommodate its cooking necessities. The ratio is 3:1.
3. Let the kamut cool down by rinsing it and set it aside.
4. Use a serving bowl of your choice and place the rest of the ingredients inside once the kamut has cooled down. Mix the ingredients together well and then serve.

# Chapter Five: Soups

When the fall and winter seasons come up, everyone is in the mood for soups and your instant pot is the best accessory to use for making your own homemade soup. Here are a few recipes that will satisfy any soup craving you may have. There are quite a variety of soups that can be cooked in your instant pot even if they are vegan. Add or ignore any added ingredients that are there for flavor. Soup is a fairly flexible recipe type that can be messed with and have little consequence most of the time if anything necessary is taken away. Feel free to play around with any flavors that you want to incorporate into your soup of choice.

All of these soups can easily be stored and used for meal planning. They have a low-calorie count but are packed full of nutrients and plenty of subtle water intake for your body. This makes any soup of your choice a great meal and healthy alternative that is convenient and can be easily taken wherever your busy day may take you. Vegan ingredients make leftovers friendly items to be stored whether you have access to a refrigerator while you are away from home or not. You won't have to worry about dairy or meat products going bad if stored in an improper way. This is just another reason that makes vegan recipes more convenient and friendly.

## Potato Soup

When you need a vegan-friendly potato soup, this recipe will be your fix. If you want your soup to be more "creamier", you can add a few your own milk alternatives like soy or almond milk. Add your own favorite herbs and feel free to focus mainly on the potatoes if you don't care for the extra vegetables that are already included. Top with your own choice of vegan-friendly cheese, sour cream, or other toppings of your choice.

This recipe will make 8 cups.

150 calories per cup

Prepping time: 15 minutes
Cooking time: 45 minutes
Total time: 1 hour

What to include:

2 pounds of potatoes that are peeled and cut into 6 pieces of each
¾ cup of baby carrots that are sliced
an 18 ounce can of Progresso creamy roasted garlic recipe starter
1 cup of onion that is chopped
1 cup vegetable broth
½ cup of celery that is chopped
½ cup of fresh baby spinach leaves that are chopped

1 tablespoon of ground flax or chia seed (this is optional for nutrition and not flavor)
½ teaspoon of salt
1/8 teaspoon of paprika
1/8 teaspoon of crushed red pepper

What to do:

1. Place all of the ingredients into your instant pot and stir together.
2. Close and lock the lid. Then press the soup button. Set the cooking time for 30 minutes. It will take about 15 minutes for the

pressure to come up so this process can take around 45 minutes itself.

3. You will then use the quick release method to release the pressure after the cooking time is done.

4. Then, use an immersion or stick blender in order to mix all the ingredients together. Do quick zaps in order to get the soup to your desired thickness. Add your desired amount of salt and then serve.

# Vegetable Soup

When you are in the mood for your fix of vegetables, this soup will do the fix. It takes little preparation and has plenty of cook time in order to let all the flavors of the ingredients mingle together. It has plenty of herbs to add great flavor and added nutrients. It is an easy recipe that you can mix and leave in your instant pot and then come back to after the cooking time is up. Add or leave out any added ingredients that you don't care for in order to alter the recipe to your own preference. This mixes well with garlic bread or cornbread.

This recipe will serve 6 people.

Prepping time: 5 minutes
Cooking time: 40 minutes
Total time: 45 minutes

Serving size: 1/6 of recipe
Calories per serving: 201

12 ounces of frozen Italian vegetables
1 15-ounce can of diced tomatoes
1 15-ounce can of cannelloni beans that are undrained
1 15-ounce can of pinto beans or kidney beans that are undrained
3 cups of water
¼ cup of quinoa that is rinsed
1 tablespoon of dried basil
1 tablespoon of garlic that is minced
1 tablespoon of hot sauce
½ tablespoon of dried oregano
1 teaspoon of onion powder
½ teaspoon of salt

¼ teaspoon of ground black pepper

What to do:

1. Add all of the ingredients to the instant pot and stir together.
2. You will then close the lid of the instant pot and lock it. Cook the soup for 2 minutes at high pressure.
3. After the cooking time is done, you will use the normal release method in order to release the pressure from the instant pot. Then, you can remove the lid and mix the soup together until it has a good consistency. Add more water or vegetable broth to get your desired consistency.
4. Season according to your own preference.

# Tomato Soup

This soup takes little time to prepare and cook. It contains more than tomato puree and ingredients. It has onions, potatoes, and carrots in the mix. There are no alternative non-dairy products added into the recipe although you could easily add your own to make it a "creamy" mixture. If you want to focus more on the tomato part of the recipe, you could easily leave out the onions, potatoes, and carrots that are in the mix. You could easily add plenty of chopped basil leaves and rosemary in order to make the classic tomato basil soup mixture. Play around with the recipe as you please. Find ways to make it your own. This, of course, will pair well with garlic bread or a grilled "cheese" sandwich to dip in the mix.

This recipe will serve 6 people.

Prepping time: 5 minutes
Cooking time: 15 minutes
Total time: 20 minutes

Calories per serving: 120

What to include:

4 cups of water
1 medium carrot that is roughly chopped
1 medium onion that is roughly sliced
1 medium potato that is roughly diced
1 28-ounce of whole canned tomatoes in their juice
4 tablespoons of vegan butter
3 rounded tablespoons of tomato paste or concentrate

3 rounded tablespoons of sun-dried tomatoes that are roughly chopped
2 teaspoons of salt
2 pinches of black pepper

What to do:

1. Pre-heat your instant pot on medium heat and keep the lid off. Then, add the butter, pepper, onions, and the carrots. Stir together the ingredients occasionally until the onions start to soften. This process should take about 5 minutes.
2. Then, add the potatoes, canned tomatoes, tomato paste, the sun-dried tomatoes, water and salt.
3. You will then close the lid of the instant pot and lock it. You will then cook the soup for 5 minutes at high pressure. After the cooking time is done, you will use the natural release method in order to release the pressure from the instant pot. Wait for the pressure to naturally come down on its own. This should take about 10 minutes. Release any remaining pressure using the normal method after 10 minutes.
4. Use an immersion blender in order to mix the ingredients to a smooth mixture, then serve.

# Black-eyed Pea Chili with Quinoa and Corn

This pairs well with chips and non-dairy sour cream. It is a great tasting Mexican style soup with plenty of protein and fiber provided in the black-eyed peas. The spices will keep you from noticing there is no meat in the chili. This soup will pair well with corn bread. Play around with the flavors as you like.

This recipe should serve 8 people.

Prepping time: 15 minutes
Cooking time: 2 hours
Total time: 2 hours and 15 minutes

Serving size: 1/8th of recipe
Calories per serving: 309


What to include:

2 large onions that are chopped
1 large green bell pepper that is chopped
1 large red bell pepper that is chopped
5 cups of fresh black-eyed peas or 2 ½ cups of dried peas soaked and drained
6 cups of vegetable broth
6 cloves of garlic that is minced
1 ½ cup of fresh or frozen corn
1/3 cup of uncooked quinoa that has been rinsed
2 15-ounce cans of diced tomatoes that are undrained
¼ to ½ teaspoon of either chipotle powder, red pepper, or hot smoked paprika
2 ½ tablespoons of mild chili powder

1 tablespoon of cocoa powder
2 teaspoons of ground cumin
2 teaspoons of smoked paprika
salt and pepper to taste
lime wedges and avocado slices are optional

What to do:

1. To start off, use the saute button on your instant pot. Then, add the onions and cook until they are soft. This process should take about 5 minutes.
2. Add the bell peppers and then continue to saute for another 3 minutes. Then, add the garlic and saute for an additional minute.
3. You will then add the black-eyed peas along with the rest of the ingredients excluding the quinoa and the corn, and any optional ingredients that can be added at the end of the cooking process. You will then close the lid of the instant pot and lock it. You will cook for 10 minutes at high pressure. You will use the natural release method in order to release the pressure after the cooking time is done.
4. After the ingredients are tender, check your seasoning to see if it fits your preference. Tweak as desired.
5. Add the corn, and quinoa and then cook until the quinoa is tender.
6. Add your optional ingredients here and serve.

# Taco Soup

This soup pairs well with cornbread. As mentioned before, the spices in the mix will keep you from noticing there is no meat in the mix. Keep the mixture warm for an extended amount of time in order to let all the flavors settle well. Add dairy-free sour cream and dairy free cheese to top of your own preference. Play around with the amounts of spices and herbs to your own desired amount.

This recipe should serve 6 people.

Prepping time: 10 minutes
Cooking time: 20 minutes
Total time: 30 minutes

Serving size: 1/6th of recipe
Calories per serving: 280

What to include:

2 15-ounce cans of black beans that are drained and rinsed
2 15-ounce cans of diced tomatoes that are undrained
2 15-ounce cans of tomato sauce
2 12-ounce cans filled with water
1 large onion that is diced
3 to 4 cloves of garlic that is minced
1 cup of frozen corn or 1 can
1 cup of frozen and chopped spinach
3 tablespoons of chili powder
1 tablespoon of paprika
½ tablespoon of cumin
¼ cup of cilantro that is diced (optional)

1 tablespoon of chipotle hot sauce (optional)
a dash of chipotle chili powder (optional)

What to do:

1. Click the saute button on your instant pot and then add the onion, garlic, and saute until it is brown. Add water if you start to notice any sticking.
2. Add the rest of the ingredients and then stir well. You will then close the lid of the instant pot and lock it. You will then cook the soup for 3 minutes at high pressure. Use the natural release method in order to release the pressure after the cooking time is done. You will want to wait for the pressure to naturally come down on its own. This should take about 10 minutes.
3. Stir well and then serve.

# Three Bean Vegan Chili

This chili is a great source of protein, especially if you cut out meat of any sort. This recipe has many different possibilities, herbs, spices, and toppings that you can add to make it your very own and catered to your desired tastes. This will give you plenty of sustainable energy even on cold, cloudy days that make you want to take a nap.

This recipe should serve 6 to 8 people.

Prepping time: 10 minutes
Cooking time: 17 minutes
Total time: 27 minutes

Calories per serving: 320

What to include:

2/3 cup of dried black beans
2/3 cup of dried pinto beans
2/3 dried red beans
2 cups of onion that is chopped
1 tablespoon of garlic that is minced
1 teaspoon of cumin seeds
3 ½ cups of water or vegetable broth
¾ cup of carrots that are chopped
¼ cup of celery that is chopped
1 red bell pepper without the seed that is chopped
2 tablespoons of mild chili powder
1 ½ teaspoon of dried oregano
1 ½ teaspoon of cumin
1 teaspoon of smoked paprika

½ teaspoon of coriander

¼ teaspoon of cayenne pepper (this is optional)

1 14-ounce can of diced tomatoes

1 14-ounce can of tomato sauce

What to do:

1. Rinse all of the beans and then combine them in a large bowl and cover with plenty of water. Allow the beans to soak for at least 8 hours. If you are using canned beans, you can easily skip this step.
2. In your instant pot, saute the cumin seeds, the onion, and minced garlic for about 5 minutes. Add vegetable broth to prevent any burning or sticking.
3. Then, you will add the rest of the ingredients that are remaining excluding the diced tomatoes and the tomato sauce. These will be added after the cooking process. You will then stir the contents well and then close the lid of the instant pot and lock it. At high pressure, cook for 12 minutes. After the cooking time is done, release the pressure using the natural release method.
4. Stir in the can of diced tomatoes and the can of tomato sauce. Allow the chili to cool, and thicken. Keep the lid off. If you desire thicker chili, blend 1 to 2 cups at high speed in a blender and then return the mixture to the pot. You can also use an immersion or stick blender to do so.
5. After you are pleased with your chili and its consistency, you can serve with any Vegan-friendly topping.

# Chapter Six: Dessert

There are plenty of great desserts to be made in your instant pot. Here are just a few that can be made in your instant pot. One of the following three recipes should fit your taste when it comes to your sweet tooth.

## Tapioca Pudding

Make your own delicious homemade vanilla, orange or lemon tapioca pudding. This is a great alternative compared to regular pudding with double or triple the amount of sugar. Plus, your pudding will be made with simple and natural ingredients. This is a much healthier alternative for anyone. You can use nut milk or coconut milk, and a sweetener of your choice. You can create different flavors by infusing the zest of an orange, lemon, or half of a vanilla pod or a teaspoon of vanilla extract. Dried or fresh fruit can also be added to create a parfait.

This recipe serves 4 to 6 people.

Prepping time: 5 minutes
Cooking time: 20 minutes
Total time: 25 minutes

Serving size: ¼th
Calories per serving: 187

What to include:

1/3 cup of tapioca pearls
1 ¼ cup of your favorite milk alternative

½ cup of water
½ cup of sugar
either ½ zested lemon or orange, or ½ vanilla bean

What to do:

1. To prepare your instant pot, add one cup of water and the steamer basket.
2. Rinse off the tapioca pearls in a strainer made up of fine mesh in order to keep all the pearls contained.
3. In a 4 cup capacity heat-proof bowl, add the tapioca, milk substitute, the water, and your choice of zest with sugar.
4. Mix the ingredients until the sugar has completely dissolved and there is no more grit-feeling left.
5. Lower the heat-proof bowl into the instant pot, close it and lock the lid. You will then cook it for 8 minutes at high pressure. Use the natural release method in order to release the pressure from the instant pot after the cooking time is done.
6. Once all the pressure has been released, let the mixture sit in the instant pot with the lid for an additional 5 minutes before opening.
7. Carefully lift the container and scoop out into serving bowls or a main bowl.
8. Use cling wrap to tightly cover and allow the tapioca to cool and refrigerate for at least 3 hours before serving. You can serve as is or add fruit toppings to make a vegan parfait.

# "Baked" Cinnamon Apples

It is no secret that cinnamon pairs with apples perfectly. Use this recipe if you are a "cinnamon apple" person. This will be the fix to your sweet tooth. It doesn't take too long to cook and it is worth any of the time that you wait for it to be finished. Your finished result will be a soft, thoroughly cooked apple with plenty of cinnamon flavor. You are able to find apples in any supermarket store at any time of the year. This is because all the apples that end up being harvested in the fall are stored in a "protective atmosphere" that will prevent them from aging. The storage of the apples can change the texture of the apple and it can turn into puree during the cooking process. In order to tell if you really have a "fresh" apple, you can tell by looking at the stem of the apple. The more green and flexible the stem is, the fresher it truly is. If the stem is brown and dry, then the apple is not truly fresh and has most likely been stored in a "protective atmosphere". By making sure that you pick out truly fresh apples, you are ensuring that your cooking efforts do not go to waste and that you end up with a great tasting dessert afterwards.

This recipe will serve 6 people.

Prepping time: 5 minutes
Cooking time: 20 minutes
Total time: 25 minutes

Serving size: 1 apple
Calories per serving: 188.7

What to include:

6 apples that are fresh and cored
¼ cup of raisins
1 cup of red wine
½ cup of raw demerara sugar
1 teaspoon of cinnamon powder

What to do:

1. Add the apples to the base of your instant pot. Pour in the wine, sprinkle the raisins, the sugar and cinnamon powder.
2. Close and lock the lid of your instant pot and cook at high pressure for 10 minutes.
3. Use the natural release method in order to release the pressure from the instant pot after the cooking time is done. Wait for the pressure to come down on its own. This should take about 10 minutes.
4. Scoop each apple out of the instant pot and serve in a small bowl with plenty of cooking liquid.

# Chocolate Fondue

If you are a chocolate fan, this recipe will work for you. Make a chocolate fondue mixture in order to dip whatever food that you desire into your own custom mixed chocolate recipe. Use skewers to dip bananas, strawberries, pretzels, cookies, or whatever vegan items you desire to be dipped in chocolate. Your instant pot might not exactly be a chocolate fountain but it can easily be used as one. Use the "warm" setting and incorporate your chocolate fountain at any party, potluck, or when you just have a craving for chocolate.

This recipe serves 2 to 4 people.

Prepping time: 1 minute
Cooking time: 10 minutes
Total time: 11 minutes

Serving size: ¼th
Calories per serving: 216

What to include:

3.5 ounces of swiss dark bittersweet chocolate
3.5 ounces of unsweetened coconut milk or any milk substitute that is unsweetened
1 teaspoon of sugar (optional)
1 teaspoon of amaretto liquor (optional)

What to do:

1. You can prepare your instant pot by placing the 2 cups of water into it and setting up the rack or trivet accessory.

2. In a small heat-proof container, you will add the chocolate by breaking it up in large pieces.

3. Then, add your favorite milk substitute, sugar, and liquor if you choose to use any. Lower into your instant pot.

4. You will then close the lid of the instant pot and lock it. Cook the mixture for 2 minutes at high pressure.

5. Use the normal release method in order to release the pressure from the instant pot after the cooking time is done.

6. Open the instant pot and tilt the lid so that the condensation will not fall into the container. Use tongs to pull out the container.

7. You can use a fork or similar utensil in order to adequately mix together the ingredients. Mix them well for about a minute. Continue to stir until the mixture becomes smooth and is no longer chunky in appearance. Remember not to mix any cold ingredients to the mixture.

8. Heat the mixture over medium heat and either serve from the instant pot or move to a fondue stand. Serve with your choice of food.

# Conclusion

Whatever you decide to cook in your instant pot, the possibilities are unlimited. Once you get used to cooking with your instant pot and are filled with creative ideas, there are plenty of recipes that you can create on your own. Add to the recipes included in this book or go off on your own and make your own special creation. Your instant pot provides a great start to any meal, especially if you are looking for quick cooking times and less energy used. You will end up with a result of well-cooked ingredients to be incorporated into any of your health-conscious meals, regardless if they are vegan, or ingredients of your choice.

There are plenty of benefits to not only owning an instant pot but by choosing a vegan lifestyle. Mixing the two together only makes a better, healthier, pair. By taking the advantage of your instant pot and healthy food choices, you can add convenience and healthier meal choices to your daily life. Take time and pride in adding whatever you desire into the recipes to make them your own. A little bit of your own touch can make a world of a difference to your taste buds and to anyone who is lucky to taste your own food creations.

For those who have a busy schedule, meal planning is a great alternative versus fast food or taking up large amounts of your day in order to cook a great meal. Your instant pot can make meal planning easier and healthier altogether. Storage is easy, and the food is healthy and already made. When your food is vegan-friendly, you don't have to worry about dairy products, or meat going bad, meaning that anything you cook can be easily stored. With more natural ingredients in your pre-prepared and planned meals, you don't have to worry too much about having a place to constantly refrigerate your food. It is recommended that you do so but it is a big bonus. This is just another plus to having a vegan diet and lifestyle.

Keep an open mind to all the ways you can incorporate your instant pot into any day, social event, or food craving you might have. Use as a warmer, saute pan, steamer, slow cooker and much more. Don't be hesitant to look for alternative cooking methods for anything that you choose to cook. Take pride in your food and your instant pot accessory helping you successfully plan and prepare your food choices. When you live a health-conscious vegan diet and lifestyle, you take pride in the ingredients you not only put in your body but also the products that you use for your body. Take pride in what you choose to nourish your body with. Owning an instant pot only helps you cook and preserve the nutrients in the ingredients you incorporate into every recipe, whether they are included in the recipe, or your own additives.

The instant pot only gives you plenty of great ways to cook your food and come up with healthy and tasteful ideas. Make sure you understand how to safely use your instant pot before completely diving into all the methods mentioned in this cookbook. Have fun and enjoy your future cooking!

# Thank You!

Thank you again for downloading this book!

I hope this book was able to help you explore the many possible meal ideas you can come up with in your instant pot whether they are by the book recipes or guidelines added with your own.

The next step is to practice using your instant pot whenever you can.

Finally, if you enjoyed this book, please take the time to share your thoughts and post a review on Amazon. It'd be greatly appreciated!

Thank you and good luck!

# Instant Pot Vegan Cookbook

*Healthy, Easy, Cheap, Delicious Vegan Instant Pot Recipes that Will Save You Time and Money!*

© Copyright 2016 by Gabriel Montana - All rights reserved.

The following eBook is reproduced below with the goal of providing information that is as accurate and reliable as possible. Regardless, purchasing this eBook can be seen as consent to the fact that both the publisher and the author of this book are in no way experts on the topics discussed within and that any recommendations or suggestions that are made herein are for entertainment purposes only. Professionals should be consulted as needed prior to undertaking any of the action endorsed herein.

This declaration is deemed fair and valid by both the American Bar Association and the Committee of Publishers Association and is legally binding throughout the United States.

Furthermore, the transmission, duplication or reproduction of any of the following work including specific information will be considered an illegal act irrespective of if it is done electronically or in print. This extends to creating a secondary or tertiary copy of the work or a recorded copy and is only allowed with express written consent from the Publisher. All additional right reserved.

The information in the following pages is broadly considered to be a truthful and accurate account of facts and as such any inattention, use or misuse of the information in question by the reader will render any resulting actions solely under their purview. There are no scenarios in which the publisher or the original author of this work can be in any fashion deemed liable for any hardship or damages that may befall them after undertaking information described herein.

Additionally, the information in the following pages is intended only for informational purposes and should thus be thought of as universal. As befitting its nature, it is presented without assurance regarding its prolonged validity or interim quality. Trademarks that are mentioned are done without written consent and can in no way be considered an endorsement from the trademark holder.

# Table of Contents

Introduction ................................................................... 1

Chapter 1: Breakfasts ................................................... 3

Chapter 2: Lunches .................................................... 16

Chapter 3: Dinners ..................................................... 31

Chapter 4: Desserts ................................................... 46

Conclusion ................................................................ 61

# Introduction

Congratulations on downloading this book and thank you for doing so.

The following chapters will discuss vegan recipes and how you can use them in your Instant Pot pressure cooker.

There are plenty of books on this subject on the market, thanks again for choosing this one! Every effort was made to ensure it is full of as much useful information as possible, please enjoy!

The Instant Pot was designed to be a pressure cooker, but you will find that it is so much more than that. The cooker has many different functions and has different settings so that you will be able to cook different things. This is something that has been made available to you so that you will be able to get the most out of it.

Using your Instant Pot will not only allow you to take a much shorter time when you are cooking, but it will also give you the many options that come along with it. The Instant Pot is designed to cook healthy food in a short amount of time and with minimal effort compared to other methods of cooking.

When you use your Instant Pot to cook the meals that you want, you will not have to worry about your kitchen getting overly hot from the oven, you'll have meals that are prepared quickly and easily, and you can help improve your overall health by cooking meals that are nutritious.

The Instant Pot Vegan Cookbook will give you all of the recipes that you need to make sure that you are right on track with where you want to be. The recipes are quick and delicious.

The best part about this cookbook is that it won't cost you a fortune to be able to eat in a way that is good for you and sustainable for the earth. No matter what your reasons are for being a vegan or if you just like vegan recipes, you can feel good about making them because they are all affordable!

We want to make sure that vegans have access to affordable recipes that they don't have to sacrifice a fortune for. This cookbook shows that having easy, healthy and affordable recipes all in one place *can* be done for vegans.

# Chapter 1: Breakfasts

If you're a vegan, you know how hard it can be to have breakfasts that are nutritious, delicious and not boring. Eating the same thing over and over can get boring and can cause you to feel like you are not getting the most out of life. Since you can't load up on greasy bacon and eggs for breakfast, try one of these recipes that will leave you feeling full, happy and without any of the guilt that comes with eating the byproducts of meat.

## Quick Oatmeal

Level of Difficulty: 1
Preparation Time: 5 minutes
Serving Size: 2 bowls of oatmeal

### You Will Need:
- Steel cut oats, 1 cup for 2-3 servings
- Water, 3 cups
- Apple pie spice, 1-2 tsp depending on tastes
- 1 large apple that has been cut up

### Appliances Needed:
Instant Pot

### Directions:
Place all of your ingredients except for the apples into your Instant Pot. Make sure that the oatmeal and the water are mixed up. Tighten the lid and close the vent on it so that no steam will escape. Set the Instant Pot to manual and set it for three minutes. It will only take that long. Turn your Instant Pot off and allow the pressure to be released from the pot so that you do not get hit with the steam. Remove the lid and top with the apples so that you've got a hot and ready breakfast.

### Notes on the Recipe:
You can use any toppings or spices for this. Fruit is always good with oatmeal but gets creative. Coconut oil and brown sugar with a pinch of salt make an excellent alternative to the traditional butter and brown sugar that is sometimes eaten in oatmeal. Raisins are also delicious in this morning oatmeal.

## Nutritional Information:

| Calories | Fat | Sodium | Carbohydrates | Fiber | Sugar |
|---|---|---|---|---|---|
| 213 | 2.9 | 3 | 43 | 6.8 | 12 |

This recipe was designed for someone who is following a vegan diet. It is, obviously, not low carb and should not be used as such. The carbohydrates that are in the oatmeal and the apple will help to keep you full for the morning, but you may want to consider some additional calories to help keep you satisfied until it is time to eat a morning snack or your lunch.

# Vegan Cocogurt

Level of Difficulty: 2
Preparation Time: 9 hours
Serving Size: 4 pints

## You Will Need:
- Coconut milk, 4 different cans or 6 boxes
- 1 small envelope of yogurt starter, dairy free option
- 4 glass pint jars with lids

## Appliances Needed:
Instant Pot
Stove

## Directions:
Pour all of your coconut milk into a sauce pan and place it on the stove. Let it heat up until it is boiling. As soon as it begins to boil, give it a good stir and pour it into the pint jars that you have already set up. They do not have to be sterilized because the boiling milk will do that job. Do not disturb them and let them cool until they no longer burn your finger but are still warm to the touch. Put the lids on the jars. Place the jars into your Instant Pot and put it on the yogurt setting. It should take around 8 hours for the yogurt to be finished.

## Notes on the Recipe:
If you have made dairy free yogurt in the past with your Instant Pot, you do not have to worry about getting a yogurt starter. You can simply use the yogurt that is left over, about 2 tablesps of it. This will work as the starter and will allow your cocogurt to be made properly.

You can top your cocogurt with anything that you want. You can also mix it after it has finished cooking in the pressure cooker. Since there is no dairy in it, there is no need to keep it refrigerated. You may want to refrigerate before you eat, though, for the best flavor possible.

**Nutritional Information:**

| Calories | Fat | Sodium | Carbohydrates | Fiber | Sugar |
|---|---|---|---|---|---|
| 245 | 3 | 6 | 5.9 | 2.3 | 3.5 |

This is a relatively low sugar snack, but the calories in it are somewhat high. For this reason, it would make a great snack or even a great breakfast or meal replacement for you to be able to enjoy as a vegan treat. The different toppings that you put on the cocogurt or mix in with it will change the nutrition.

# Fall Fruit Crisp

Level of Difficulty: 1
Preparation Time: 15 minutes
Serving Size: 4

**You Will Need:**
- Fruit that is cut into chunks, 2 pears, and 3 apples
- 1 cup of oatmeal that is steel cut
- ¼ of a cup of brown sugar
- 1 ½ of a cup of water that is hot but not boiling
- ½ of a tsp of cinnamon or apple pie spice

**Appliances Needed:**
Instant Pot

**Directions:**
Once you have cut all of your ingredients up into the same size and they are ready for you to be able to put into the pot, mix them up inside of the pot. Make sure that they are incorporated and that there are no big chunks of sugar that are sitting on top or inside of any of the fruit. The water should help to mix up the sugar that is in the recipe and will help it to incorporate with the fruit better. The recipe will taste better if it is all thoroughly mixed up. Close your Instant Pot and make sure that the vent is shut. Use the manual function of the Instant Pot to be able to set it to 12 minutes. Cook your food until it is done with the 12 minutes. Turn it off and let the pressure release before you open. Serve warm. Reheat if necessary.

**Notes on the Recipe:**
Not only will this recipe make a great breakfast for anyone who wants the warm and delicious taste of fall but it will also

work as a dessert or a snack. It is a recipe that only tastes bad. If you are trying to avoid using sugar, you can replace it with agave nectar or any other natural vegan sweetener. Try to avoid using artificial sweeteners because of the health problems that they have the potential to cause.

**Nutritional Information:**

| Calories | Fat | Sodium | Carbohydrates | Fiber | Sugar |
|---|---|---|---|---|---|
| 272 | 1.8 | 4 | 65 | 9.4 | 14 |

The recipe has low fat, but it is high in carbohydrates and sugar. This can be used to your advantage, and you can use it as a recipe that is able to keep you feeling very full throughout the day.

# Scrambled Tofu and Potatoes

Level of Difficulty: 1
Preparation Time: 20 minutes
Serving Size: 2

## You Will Need:
- 1 block of small tofu that has been cut into small pieces
- 2 potatoes that have been peeled and cut into small pieces
- Southwest seasoning
- Pepper and salt
- 1 tsp of coconut oil
- ¼ of a cup of water

## Appliances Needed:
Instant Pot

## Directions:
Once you have cut up your potatoes so that they are diced, and your tofu is in small pieces that slightly resemble that of scrambled eggs, you can begin adding everything to your Instant Pot. Make sure that you mix it up as much as possible before you start to cook it to ensure that you are getting all of the flavors mixed together. You can use melted or not melted coconut oil for this recipe. Put the lid onto your Instant Pot and set it so that it is on the manual function. Cook for 10 minutes. The potatoes should be tender but should not be to the point that they would be able to be mashed. Make sure that you let the pressure release naturally before you take it out of the Instant Pot.

## Notes on the Recipe:

If you do not want to use the Southwest seasoning for this or you want to use other spices that are more to your liking, you can add a different flavor to the dish. It will be easier to make if you know what you like. You can also add anything else to it including onions and peppers which will give it an entirely different flavor. No matter what you add, make sure that everything is around the same size when you cut it up. This will make it easier to cook and consume.

## Nutritional Information:

| Calories | Fat | Sodium | Carbohydrates | Fiber | Sugar |
|---|---|---|---|---|---|
| 206 | 4.8 | 12 | 34 | 5.6 | 2.8 |

This recipe is great for breakfast or at the base of many different dinner and lunch recipes. The fat in it is due to the coconut oil and can be changed. If you add ingredients to the recipe, the nutritional information will also change.

## Porridge that is Made with Buckwheat

Level of Difficulty: 2
Preparation Time: 15 minutes
Serving Size: 4

**You Will Need:**
- Buckwheat that is not shredded, 1 cup
- Rice milk or another milk substitute, 3 cups
- 1 sliced up banana
- ¼ of a cup of raisins
- 1 ½ of a tsp of cinnamon
- ½ of a tsp of vanilla
- Nuts for topping

**Appliances Needed:**
Instant Pot

**Directions:**
Make sure that the buckwheat is on the bottom of your Instant Pot. Begin by adding all of the other ingredients on top of it and stir to combine but do not mix too much. Close the lid on your Instant Pot and make sure that the vent is closed on the lid. This will keep the steam from releasing while you are cooking the buckwheat. For this recipe, you will continue to use the manual setting and put it at 6 minutes. The porridge will be done in the 6 minutes, but you should let it sit for around 8-10 minutes after you have turned it off so that it has time for the pressure to release out of the pot.

**Notes on the Recipe:**
You don't have to use a banana in this recipe. Any fruit will work, and you can even use cranberries in place of the

raisins. Choose your favorite type of nut to put on the top. If you are using the banana and raisin recipe, it is especially good with walnuts on top. The nuts on top are helpful because they can help give you energy that will keep you pushing through the midmorning snack time and all the way until it is time to eat lunch.

**Nutritional Information:**

| Calories | Fat | Sodium | Carbohydrates | Fiber | Sugar |
|---|---|---|---|---|---|
| 292 | 6.2 | 66 | 33 | 2.6 | 9.1 |

If you make any adjustments to the recipe or add any other type of fruit, the nutritional information will change. Most fruit should be around the same when it comes to calories and sugar, but they will all have different amounts of fiber in them. Berries have more fiber than other fruits.

# Fake Chocolate Pudding

Level of Difficulty: 2
Preparation Time: 9 hours
Serving Size: 16

**You Will Need:**
- Coconut milk, 4 different cans or 6 boxes
- 1 small envelope of yogurt starter, dairy free option
- ¼ of a cup of cocoa powder
- ¼ of a cup of raspberries
- 4 glass pint jars with lids

**Appliances Needed:**
Instant Pot
Stove

**Directions:**
Pour all of your coconut milk into a sauce pan and place it on the stove. Let it heat up until it is boiling. As soon as it begins to boil, give it a good stir and pour it into the pint jars that you have already set up. They do not have to be sterilized because the boiling milk will do that job. Do not disturb them and let them cool until they no longer burn your finger but are still warm to the touch. Mix in the cocoa powder so that the mixture takes on a brown color and appears to be chocolate pudding. Put the lids on the jars. Place the jars into your Instant Pot and put it on the yogurt setting. It should take around 8 hours for the yogurt to be finished. You can top with fresh raspberries or any other fruit.

## Notes on the Recipe:

To give it one extra layer of flavor that will be good for you to use, put some vanilla extract in it to make it taste even sweeter and creamier. The yogurt does not need to be topped with raspberries or anything at all and will still have a rich chocolate flavor to it. If you have made the plain cocogurt before using your Instant Pot, you can use that instead of a commercial starter. Just be sure to always save around 1-2 tbsp of cocogurt back each time you make it so that you don't have to worry about buying a starter. Top with strawberries to try something that tastes just like chocolate covered strawberries for breakfast. This may not taste like the most nutritional breakfast, but it is so much more than just a sweet treat. The calorie count and carbohydrates will keep you full until lunch time and beyond. You can also use this for a nutritious sweet treat that you don't have to feel guilty about.

## Nutritional Information:

| Calories | Fat | Sodium | Carbohydrates | Fiber | Sugar |
|---|---|---|---|---|---|
| 245 | 3 | 6 | 5.9 | 2.3 | 3.5 |

# Chapter 2: Lunches

Lunch is so much more than just the time where you get to take a breather at the office. Make sure that you are getting the most out of your lunchtime routine by whipping up one of these great recipes in your Instant Pot. Busy week ahead? Make the recipes ahead of time in your Instant Pot, toss them in a container and take them to work with you. The only thing you'll need is a microwave to heat them up while you are at work.

All of the recipes are designed to be eaten on their own, but they can also be served with other ingredients for a lunch that has many options to it. Always consider the nutritional information and whether or not it will give you the full filling that you need to keep you satisfied until dinnertime.

## Curry with Lentils

Level of Difficulty: 2
Preparation Time: 25 minutes
Serving Size: 4

### You Will Need:
- Coconut milk, 1 can
- Dry lentils, any color, 2 cups of them
- 1 large can of fire roasted tomatoes that are crushed
- 1 onion that has been diced
- 1 small tin can of tomato paste
- Garlic that has been minced – 4 cloves or 2 tbsp
- Minced ginger 1 tsp
- 2 tbsp of vegetable base or broth
- Water, 5 cups
- 2 ½ tbsp of curry powder or paste
- ½ of a tsp of paprika
- 1 cup of frozen spinach that is chopped

### Appliances Needed:
Instant Pot
Stove

### Directions:
Make sure that all of your ingredients are chopped and prepared prior to getting started with the recipe. Add the onion and the garlic along with the spinach to a sauce pan and cook over medium heat. Do it until the onions turn translucent. Add that and the rest of your ingredients to your Instant Pot. Make sure that they are all mixed up to incorporate the flavors. Put your Instant Pot on the manual setting and cook for 15 minutes. This will be enough time to soften the lentils to the point that you can eat them. Let the pressure release naturally.

### Notes on the Recipe:

You can eat this plain or serve it with a combination of rice and vegetables. For an extra wonderful treat, serve it with jasmine rice that has been cooked to the point that it is sweet. The spicy curry will combine well with a sweet and sticky rice mixture. This is a great recipe to make on a cold day and will be sure to keep you as warm as you would like. The curry is filling like a soup.

### Nutritional Information:

| Calories | Fat | Sodium | Carbohydrates | Fiber | Sugar |
|---|---|---|---|---|---|
| 338 | 112 | 112 | 28 | 4.3 | 12 |

# Filling Vegetable Soup

Level of Difficulty: 1
Preparation Time: 20 minutes
Serving Size: 6

## You Will Need:
- Water, 3 cups of boiling
- 12 oz frozen Italian vegetables
- 12 oz frozen California vegetables
- 1/4 of a tsp of ground black pepper
- ¼ of a cup of quinoa, pre rinsed
- 1/2 of a tsp salt
- ½ of tbsp oregano that is dried
- 1 tbsp onion powder
- 1 tbsp hot sauce
- 1 tbsp garlic, minced
- 1 tbsp dried basil
- 1 tin can pinto beans, kidney beans that are 15 oz don't drain
- 1 tin can dice tomatoes fire roasted
- 1 tin can cannelloni beans that are 15 oz don't drain

## Appliances Needed:
Instant Pot

## Directions:
Make sure that all of your ingredients that you cut up are around the same size so that you don't have to worry about what you are going to do or how long each individual vegetable needs to be cooked for. Place all of the ingredients into your Instant Pot. You can use the Instant Pot or your stove to boil the water but make sure that it is boiled so that you can begin cooking your other ingredients for a longer time. Set the pot on the soup function and allow it to cook. It should not take long before

all of the ingredients are incorporated together, and they are ready to be eaten. Be careful of the steam when you are taking the lid off of the Instant Pot.

**Notes on the Recipe:**
You can either use this with the vegetables that are recommended, or you can choose to use the vegetables that you prefer. Keep in mind that any time you change the ingredients to a recipe, the nutritional information will also change so be aware of that. Consider using vegetables that are lower in calories or carbohydrates for an option that is slightly healthier. This recipe serves 6, but you can easily get 8 helpings out of it if you make sure that they are small.

**Nutritional Information:**

| Calories | Fat | Sodium | Carbohydrates | Fiber | Sugar |
|---|---|---|---|---|---|
| 166 | 7 | 200 | 13 | 4 | 3 |

# Hummus Dip

Level of Difficulty: 1
Preparation Time: 20
Serving Size: 10

**You Will Need:**
- 2 tin cans of chickpeas do not drain or rinse
- ½ of a tbsp of minced garlic
- ½ of a tbsp of tahini paste
- Other flavorings that you may want

**Appliances Needed:**

Instant Pot

Food processor

**Directions:**

Put all of your ingredients into the Instant Pot. If you want to make more, then you can double or triple the recipe so that you can share with friends or at a party. Make sure that the lid is on tight and that the vent is completely closed and cook for 10 minutes using the manual setting. The chickpeas should get significantly softer once you have started to cook them and once they have been completely cooked. Take everything out of the Instant Pot and let cool for around 10 minutes. Place it into your food processor and make sure that it is completely mixed. Cooking the chickpeas before hand will allow you to make sure that they are not clumpy and that your hummus is much smoother.

**Notes on the Recipe:**

Many people choose to eat hummus just on its own, but it was originally intended to be a dip. You can dip your favorite vegan toasted bread into it, crackers or even vegetables. To get the most out of the hummus, make sure that you eat it within a week of cooking it and store in the refrigerator. You will be able to use it in recipes. While the traditional commercial grade hummus is vegan, there have been issues in the past with the edibility of it. It is also much more expensive. You can make double the amount of hummus for around $2.50 depending on where you live. If you buy the commercial hummus, you will pay at least $4 for a small container that contains much less than what you would be able to make on your own. There are no preservatives in this version and you can use even chickpeas that are organic to make it an even healthier option.

**Nutritional Information:**

| Calories | Fat | Sodium | Carbohydrates | Fiber | Sugar |
|---|---|---|---|---|---|
| 111 | 1.8 | 256 | 19 | 3.9 | 0 |

This sugar free snack dip mix is great for anyone who is watching what they eat. Even vegans can go sugarfree sometimes. Since the beans, the garlic, and the paste do not contain any sugar, it is a great option to keep things all natural without having to use any type of artificial sweeteners. It is just naturally sugar free. An excellent option for the diabetic person who is trying to eat vegan.

## Thanksgiving Sweet Potatoes

Level of Difficulty: 2
Preparation Time: 20 minutes
Serving Size: 10

### You Will Need:
- 4 sweet potatoes or yams that are medium-large
- ½ of a cup of coconut milk
- 1 teasp of vanilla extract
- ¼ of a cup of OJ
- ¼ of a cup of sugar
- ¼ of a cup of maple syrup
- ½ of a teasp of salt
- ½ of a teasp of nutmeg
- ½ of a teasp of cinnamon

### Appliances Needed:
Instant Pot

### Directions:
Take the skins off of all but 2 of the sweet potatoes and place everything into your Instant Pot. Put the Instant Pot on the high pressure function and cook for 10 minutes or until the potatoes are mashable. Depending on the size of the potatoes, you may have to cook it for slightly longer than the 10 minutes. Once they are done, take a masher to them or mix them up by using your hand mixer. This will incorporate all of the ingredients and will allow you the chance to make sure that they are all mixed up. You can top them with walnuts, or you can make a glaze out of water, brown sugar and walnuts to top the potatoes with.

**Notes on the Recipe:**

No marshmallows in this recipe! Since this is a vegan recipe, it is perfect for if you are asked to bring something to Thanksgiving dinner. This will allow you to show your doubtful friends and family that food *can* be delicious even if it doesn't have any nasty meat products in it. This is also a great addition to any lunch time. You can use it as a side dish at Thanksgiving, or you can use it on your own and treat it as the main dish if you are just eating lunch at work on a random Tuesday. You can also add other spices to make the dish more savory or even consider using regular potatoes to make it one that is completely savory.

**Nutritional Information:**

| Calories | Fat | Sodium | Carbohydrates | Fiber | Sugar |
|---|---|---|---|---|---|
| 298 | 13 | 195 | 44 | 3.5 | 29 |

As you can see from the nutritional information, this may not be the most healthy recipe out there. The high calorie, fat and sugar content will make it filling, though. Sweet potatoes are packed with essential nutrients, too so that you can feel not as guilty about consuming all of those calories with this fun meal.

# Happy Tacos

Level of Difficulty: 1
Preparation Time: 10 minutes
Serving Size: 4

**You Will Need:**
- 1 tin can of black beans
- 1 tin can of kidney beans
- 1 tin can of corn
- 1 glass jar of organic salsa that is vegan
- 1 small envelope of taco seasoning
- 1 head of iceberg lettuce

**Appliances Needed:**
Instant Pot

**Directions:**
Put your first four ingredients into your Instant Pot. Mix the ingredients so that they are varied and that it is colorful. Stir in the envelope of taco seasoning and make sure that all of the beans and corn are covered. If you want to make the tacos spicy, you can add some hot sauce or even some jalapenos to the mix so that it is able to be spicy the way that you like it. You can also mix two envelopes of taco seasoning together so that you are able to make a more flavorful meal. Cook in the instant pot on the manual setting for around 5 minutes. The beans should get tender, and the entire mixture should be flavorful when you are done mixing it up. Release the pressure and let it sit for a few minutes so that the steam does not burn you. Be careful when you are removing the lid of the pot. Lay your lettuce out and scoop the ingredients onto pieces of lettuce. This should make about 4 tacos but can make

much more if you decide that you want more. Double the recipe if you need to. The lettuce may not stay together too well so use a toothpick on it if you need to.

## Notes on the Recipe:

Tacos are all about what you want and the way that you like to eat them. You can make these tacos your own. If you like certain flavors, consider adding them to the mix. Tacos are always good with Southwest seasoning. You can also add fresh onions, tomatoes, and peppers to make it more appealing. Consider some of the vegan options like soy cheese and even vegan sour cream to top this with. These can get expensive, though, so use this as a recipe that is cheaper than your typical taco recipe with all of the extra toppings.

## Nutritional Information:

| Calories | Fat | Sodium | Carbohydrates | Fiber | Sugar |
|---|---|---|---|---|---|
| 302 | 10 | 156 | 38 | 12 | 5 |

The nutritional information is provided for this recipe only. If you add any of the additional ingredients that are mentioned, your nutritional information will change and will likely go up. Different brands of ingredients, like the beans, may have slightly different macro nutrient counts.

# Creamy Potato Soup

Level of Difficulty: 1
Preparation Time: 15 minutes
Serving Size: 6

**You Will Need:**
- 4 large baking potatoes that have been peeled and cut up into small chunks that will be able to be eaten easily in the soup
- 1 cup of vegetable broth
- ½ of a cup of soy milk
- 1 cup of imitation bacon
- ¼ of a cup of liquid smoke
- ¼ of a cup of tofu
- ½ of a tsp of onion powder
- ½ of a tsp of garlic powder

**Appliances Needed:**
Instant Pot

**Directions:**
Once you have cut up the potatoes, mix them with the seasonings and stir them to combine. To make sure that the flavors are combined, put them in the fridge overnight, but this is not necessary to do the recipe. Add the potatoes and the rest of the ingredients that you have to your Instant Pot. Put the lid on and close the vent on the pot so that the steam does not escape. Cook using the soup function. The soup should be liquid, but the potatoes should still be chunky. If they are not tender and easy to eat, use the manual function to cook it for another 5 minutes. This should ensure that they are tender and they are easy to eat when you are trying to eat the soup. Turn the pot off and let it release pressure for around 10

minutes. When you take the lid off of the pot, make sure that you do not get burnt by the steam. Angle the lid so that it does not hurt your arm or your hand.

**Notes on the Recipe:**
Most of the imitation bacon that is name brand and available at your local supermarket does not contain any actual animal ingredients. Check the one at your local store to make sure that it doesn't because different brands may use different methods. For the most part, liquid smoke will also be vegan but, again, check it to make sure that it does not contain any animal products. There can be hidden animal products in any of the food that you buy, even in the vegetable broth. To make sure that it is completely vegan, make your own vegetable broth at home using your Instant Pot.

**Nutritional Information:**

| Calories | Fat | Sodium | Carbohydrates | Fiber | Sugar |
|---|---|---|---|---|---|
| 276 | 12 | 303 | 48 | 7.2 | 10 |

# Popping Corn

Level of Difficulty: 1
Preparation Time: 10 minutes
Serving Size: 10

## You Will Need:
- 2 cups of popcorn kernels, any color
- 1 tbsp of coconut oil or another vegan oil
- ½ of a tsp of garam masala
- ½ of a tsp of curry powder
- ¼ of a tsp of ginger
- 1 tsp of garlic powder
- ½ of a tsp of onion powder
- ½ of a tsp of turmeric

## Appliances Needed:
Instant Pot

## Directions:
Mix your spices with coconut oil that has been melted already. This will ensure that the oil is flavored and that it will be able to pass the flavor onto the popcorn kernels. Add the kernels to the oil so that they are coated with the flavored oil and so that they are able to pick up the flavors that are in the oil. This will allow the popcorn to be more flavorful once it is cooked in the pressure cooker. Put all of the ingredients into the Instant Pot and put the lid on it. Put it on the high pressure function and cook for 5 minutes. The popcorn will pop, and things will probably be really loud during that time, but that is what it is supposed to be doing. Eat the popcorn within one day of making it so that it does not get stale and not good to eat.

**Notes on the Recipe:**

This is a recipe for Indian popcorn that has a lot of other flavors mixed in with it. The sky is the limit when it comes to your popcorn, though. You can make any flavor that you want by using your Instant Pot and your imagination. It is important to make sure that you use something that you like. You can even use sugar so that it tastes like kettle corn. Use your Instant Pot to make popcorn for yourself, for your friends and for your family.

**Nutritional Information:**

| Calories | Fat | Sodium | Carbohydrates | Fiber | Sugar |
|---|---|---|---|---|---|
| 31 | 1 | 1 | 6.2 | 1.2 | 0 |

Popcorn is a great treat and can even be used as a snack. It is included in the lunch section because it is really filling and it can be used in place of lunch. Since there are so few calories in it, it is a great option for people who are counting calories, but it will not be the best option to eat for lunch everyday. Try to make sure that you are not starving yourself by eating only popcorn for lunch because this could become a problem. Use it as a snack or in addition to one of our other great lunch recipes.

# Chapter 3: Dinners

For many people, dinner is the biggest meal that they will eat all day. It is also the time when most families get together to eat their meals so that they will be able to enjoy it together. Many times, not everyone in the family is vegan which can make it hard to be able to serve something that everyone likes. These recipes will incorporate the vegan ingredients with some of the best flavors. They can help get everyone to eat the same dinner at the same time and with the same people. They are easy to make, inexpensive, delicious and can be done in the Instant Pot for a quicker dinner.

# Risotto with Butternut Squash

Level of Difficulty: 1
Preparation Time: 20 minutes
Serving Size: 4

### You Will Need:
- 1 butter nut squash that has been cut up
- 1 ½ of a cup of risotto or regular rice
- ½ of a cup of white cooking wine
- A pinch of salt
- A pinch of pepper
- ½ of a tbsp of minced garlic
- ½ of a tbsp of cilantro
- 1 bag of spinach
- 1 small container of Portobello mushrooms
- 1 onion that has been chopped
- 3 1/2 of cups of vegetable broth or equal amount of water
- 1 chopped bell pepper
- ½ of a cup of parsley

### Appliances Needed:
Instant Pot

### Directions:
Before you begin putting the recipe together, make sure that you cut the ingredients so that they are all roughly the same size. Make sure that they have been cut and that there are no big parts that are different from the rest of them. Combine everything into the Instant Pot and mix it together so that all of the spices that are in it are able to coat the vegetables and the risotto. This is important to make sure that it is as flavorful as possible and that it gets the taste that you want. Set your Instant Pot to cook on the high pressure setting for 10 minutes. If it is done and the rice is not fully cooked, cook it for another 5 minutes or

until the rice is as tender as possible. Do not cook so long the the ingredients become mushy. Once it has been fully cooked, remove the lid and allow the steam to come out of it without getting harmed by the steam.

**Notes on the Recipe:**

The vegetables and the spices that are included in this recipe are intended to blend well together, but you can use any type of vegetables or spices that you have on hand. The recipe on its own is bursting with flavor and will be very tasty even for your family members who are not vegans and who do not normally eat vegan dinners. This can work as a dump dinner, and you can just put whatever you have on hand into the risotto to make a flavor that is completely unique. Make sure that you only include things that you enjoy. While the main parts of the recipe, like the rice and the broth, are important to keep the same, you can change it in any other way that you want to suit your own individual tastes.

**Nutritional Information:**

| Calories | Fat | Sodium | Carbohydrates | Fiber | Sugar |
|---|---|---|---|---|---|
| 423 | 10 | 159 | 56 | 12 | 16 |

This is a filling dinner that has several elements to it. You can eat it by itself, or you can serve it as the main dish, but the combination of vegetables and grains that are in it should be enough to keep you feeling full.

# Chinese Cauliflower

Level of Difficulty: 3
Preparation Time: 20 minutes
Serving Size: 4

## You Will Need:
- One head of cauliflower that is separated with stems removed
- 1 green onion that has been chopped up
- ½ of a cup of soy sauce
- ½ of a cup of sesame oil
- ¼ of a cup of chili sauce or 1 tbsp of chili powder
- 1 tsp of salt
- 1 tsp of pepper

## Appliances Needed:
Instant Pot

## Directions:
Put your cauliflower into your Instant Pot and put all of the rest of the ingredients on top of it. Stir to make sure that the cauliflower is coated and that the sauce is somewhat sticky that is coating it. This will ensure that the flavors get into the cauliflower and that it tastes good like the way that it is supposed to. Put your Instant Pot onto the poultry function because the cauliflower will be about the same consistency as the poultry that you would traditionally use. Make sure that the lid is closed and that the vent is secured. It will take around 15 minutes total for the mixture to cook.

## Notes on the Recipe:
You may be surprised that this does not taste that different from Chinese takeout. The texture is even the same.

Cauliflower heads make an excellent substitute for chicken in many different recipes that call for you to use chicken. With this, you can serve it over a bed of white rice, with noodles that have been cooked Chinese style or even over your favorite another type of grain. It is also great to eat on its own and can be very filling when you are looking for something that is a great treat to eat or when you are craving something that may not be the healthiest thing.

**Nutritional Information:**

| Calories | Fat | Sodium | Carbohydrates | Fiber | Sugar |
|---|---|---|---|---|---|
| 241 | 8 | 356 | 4 | 10 | 4 |

Note that the nutritional information may vary depending on the ingredients that you use. For example, if you use chili sauce instead of chili powder, you will have more calories than sugar, but you will also have a stickier consistency to make it taste more authentic. The nutritional information may vary, also, depending on the brand of sauce that you use and the way that you use it. You can make sure that your nutritional information is accurate by always checking it before you cook and making sure that it is in line with what you think the recipe will be.

# Asian Style Sesame Noodles

Level of Difficulty: 1
Preparation Time: 10 minutes
Serving Size: 2

## You Will Need:
- 1 box of spaghetti noodles that are vegan
- ½ of a cup of sesame oil
- ½ of a cup of soy sauce
- 3 cups of water that has been heated up but is not boiling

## Appliances Needed:
Instant Pot

## Directions:
Put your noodles into your Instant Pot. You may need to break them in half so that they will fit horizontally into the pot but you can also purchase a box that is "pot sized." Once they are in your pan, cover them with the three cups of water and make sure that all of the noodles are fully submerged in the water. Put the lid on the pot and close the vent so that the steam cannot escape. Set it on high pressure for 5 minutes. It may take a few minutes for the pot to build up the pressure that it needs to be able to cook the noodles, but they should be done and tender in no time. Make sure that you are careful when you take the lid off so that you do not burn yourself. Remove the lid, then remove the noodles from the pot. Put the noodles into a different bowl and coat them with the sesame oil and the soy sauce.

**Notes on the Recipe:**

If you are making another one of the Chinese recipes in this book or that you know of, you can use these noodles to serve the recipe on. They are also great for eating just on their own, but they may not give you the nutrition that you need to be satisfied after you eat dinner. Consider adding vegetables to the noodles to give them a lot more taste and to make them have more nutritional value so that you can enjoy them as your only meal. It is a good idea to add vegetables to the noodles before you cook them in the Instant Pot, so they will get tender at the same time and so that you do not have to worry about cooking the vegetables in a separate pot or on the stove where you will make more of a mess while you are cooking.

**Nutritional Information:**

| Calories | Fat | Sodium | Carbohydrates | Fiber | Sugar |
|---|---|---|---|---|---|
| 280 | 6 | 358 | 29 | 13 | 10 |

There are many different things that could factor into the nutrition of this dish. Different brands of noodles may cause the dish to go up or down in each of the nutritional categories. You can also consider using all vegetable noodles to be sure that you are getting the lowest amount of calories possible. Be sure to look for noodles that are labeled as strictly vegan so that you don't have to worry about eggs that could be in the noodles or other ingredients that may not be friendly to the vegan diet that you are trying to stay on while you are eating different types of food.

# Spaghetti

Level of Difficulty: 3
Preparation Time: 1 hour
Serving Size: 4

**You Will Need:**
- 1 spaghetti squash
- A small pinch of salt and pepper
- 1 tin can of diced tomatoes
- ½ of a tsp of garlic
- ½ of a tsp of Italian seasoning
- 1 tsp of oregano
- 1 tsp of basil
- 1 full cup of water

**Appliances Needed:**

Instant Pot

**Directions:**

Start out by cutting your spaghetti squash in half from the top to the bottom. Take the seeds out of it and make sure that there is no debris inside of it. Rub down each side of it with salt and pepper, on the fleshy sides. Place it into your pressure cooker. If you cannot fit it into the pressure cooker, you can cut it in half again across the middle of it. Make sure that the lid will fit on top without being crooked or fall off. Lock it into place and close the steam valve to ensure that the steam does not come out of it while you are cooking. Put the pressure cooker onto the manual function and cook for 20 minutes or until it is tender. Allow the Instant Pot to depressurize before you try to take the lid off so that you do not get hurt by the steam or the pressure that comes out of the pot.

Take a fork and scrape the insides of the squash out and back into the Instant Pot. It should come off easily, and it should look like spaghetti when it comes apart. It should come off in long strings and should be easy to get out. Scrape it until you get to the outside of the spaghetti squash. Put the rest of the ingredients into the pot and stir up so that they are well combined. Put the Instant Pot onto the soup function. It should cook for another 5 or so minutes until it is done. Take it out and serve.

**Notes on the Recipe:**

There are many substitutes for cheese that are available for vegans. You can top it with soy cheese, or you can leave it how it is to save the money that you would spend on cheese. You can also purchase or make meatless meatballs to top it off, but again, you can also avoid that and save some money. Make sure that you serve it while it is hot. Spaghetti squash does not taste the greatest when it is reheated but if you do choose to save it for leftovers make sure that you eat it within one day of cooking it so that it tastes the best. This recipe is especially good when you serve it with a small side salad of lettuce, tomato, olive oil and vinegar but you can also eat it on its own.

**Nutritional Information:**

| Calories | Fat | Sodium | Carbohydrates | Fiber | Sugar |
|---|---|---|---|---|---|
| 113 | 0 | 139 | 6 | 12 | 4.3 |

The size of your spaghetti squash and the portions that you decide to dish out will dictate the nutritional information. For the most part, your tomatoes should not vary too much but check the nutritional information because some brands can be many more calories than other brands. It is a good idea to make sure that you are consistent each time that you make this so that you do not have to worry about the different nutritional information and what it is doing to the recipe. Adding vegan meatballs or soy cheese to the top of it will drastically increase the calorie count of the recipe.

# Creamless Creamy Tomato Soup

Level of Difficulty: 1
Preparation Time: 20 minutes
Serving Size: 4

**You Will Need:**
- 1 large tin can of tomato paste
- 1 large tin can of whole tomatoes
- 2 full cups of water
- 1 cup of vegetable broth
- ½ of a cup of cashews or cashew pieces
- ¼ of a cup of oats
- 1 tbsp of basil
- 2 tbsp of garlic that has been minced

**Appliances Needed:**
Instant Pot
Food processor

**Directions:**
Put all of the ingredients that you have gathered into your Instant Pot. Do not drain the liquid out of the tin cans. Once they have all been put into the pot and they are all mixed together, you can secure the lid on the top of the Instant Pot. Make sure that the vent is closed before you start cooking because it will not be able to build up pressure if you leave the vent open. You can put it on the soup function, and it will cook in about 10 minutes. If you put it on the high pressure function, it will cook in 10 minutes, but it will also make sure that the tomatoes are completely incorporated. Let the pressure release and remove the lid from the top of the pot. Let it sit for a few minutes or until it cools down. Put it in a food processor to make sure that it is soup like and that all of the ingredients

are well blended. There should be no chunks. After you have blended it all up, heat it back up either in the microwave or on the stove. Heat only until it is as hot as you want it and be sure that you don't make it too hot so that you can't eat it.

### Notes on the Recipe:

There are some crackers that come in vegan varieties so that you can add them to the top of your soup. You can also eat this with vegan grilled soy cheese or another substitute for the regular cheese that would be in it. There are many options that you can do with this soup. While the soup goes great with a lot of different things, it also works well on its own. It has enough in it so that it is filling on its own without the addition of any sides to it.

### Nutritional Information:

| Calories | Fat | Sodium | Carbohydrates | Fiber | Sugar |
|---|---|---|---|---|---|
| 300 | 4 | 112 | 15 | 9 | 6 |

If you want to make just tomato soup without the creaminess aspect, take the cashews out of the recipe and eliminate the oats. The cashews and the oats bring a little bit of extra nutrition to the soup and also allow it to be creamier. The soup will not be affected if you make a choice to take the cashews or the oats out of it, it just won't be as creamy and will have fewer calories.

# Broccoli "Cheese" Soup

Level of Difficulty: 1
Preparation Time: 20 minutes
Serving Size: 4

**You Will Need:**
- An entire head of broccoli cut into bite pieces
- An entire head of cauliflower cut into bite pieces
- 1 tin can of white beans, do not drain them
- 1 large container of vegetable broth
- 2 carrots that have been sliced or diced into small pieces
- ¾ of a cup of coconut milk
- 1 tsp of garlic powder
- 1 tsp of salt
- 1 tsp of thyme
- 1 tsp of black pepper

**Appliances Needed:**
Instant Pot

**Directions:**
Make sure that all of your ingredients are cut into small pieces that will mix well together and will not be large in the soup. The smaller they are, the better but if you cut them until they are too small, it will be impossible to distinguish their flavor in the soup. Once they have been completely cut up, you can add all of the ingredients into your Instant Pot. You may want to make sure that you have used some cooking spray on the pot to make sure that the soup is not going to stick to it when you try to get it out but it should be fine without it. Seal the lid onto the pot and fully close the vent. Cook using the soup function for around 10 minutes. Once the Instant Pot has finished cooking, and the soup is done, turn the pot off so that you

do not have to worry about depressurizing it. It should become depressurized in about 10 minutes, and you can then remove the lid. Do so slowly and at an angle so that you do not burn your arm on the hot lid or the steam that comes out of the pot when you take it off. Serve hot.

**Notes on the Recipe:**
The ingredients in this soup combine to form a cheesy mixture that is much more than just cheesy soup. Despite the taste, it has no dairy in it and is fully vegan (and healthy!) Just be sure that you use the ingredients exactly how they are specified so that you make a soup that is creamy and delicious. This recipe will be sure to full even the biggest dairy lover in your family. The soup tastes almost no different from the way that traditional broccoli cheese soup tastes. Serve this with small squares of vegan bread or even with your favorite meal. Make sure that you use the soup within one day of making it and always refrigerate leftovers to keep the coconut milk in it from spoiling.

**Nutritional Information:**

| Calories | Fat | Sodium | Carbohydrates | Fiber | Sugar |
|---|---|---|---|---|---|
| 214 | 7.8 | 648 | 22 | 13 | 3.6 |

You can eliminate the white beans from the recipe or use another type of bean. The white beans make it have a little more of a taste to it, and they also help to make it more filling for anyone who is eating only that for dinner. Changing the type of bean will not change the soup or the recipe at all, it will only make the soup have a slightly different taste and a distinctively different color that does *not* look like traditional broccoli cheddar soup.

# Chapter 4: Desserts

Desserts can help you out with your diet by giving you the opportunity to have something that is tasty and "bad" for you once in a while, but it can be hard to find desserts that really do the trick when you're vegan. While there are plenty of natural options, like berries and sweeteners, it is still nice to be able to mix up a cake once in a while. These vegan desserts are all designed to be able to work with your Instant Pot and will have your mouth watering with the tasty ingredients that they all have. The desserts are easy to make, cheap to buy the ingredients and will give you that right amount of satisfaction.

The only guilt you'll be feeling when you make any one of these desserts is the guilt that you didn't try it out sooner!

# Holiday Cake

Level of Difficulty: 3
Preparation Time: 35 minutes
Serving Size: 8

**You Will Need:**
- 1 ½ of a cup of water
- 1 entire cup of chopped up pears
- ½ of a cup of cranberries, dried or fresh
- 2 tbsp melted coconut oil
- 2 tbsp of flax seeds that are ground up
- ¼ of a cup of natural vegan sweetener
- ½ of a cup of unsweet coconut milk
- 1/8 of a tsp of salt
- 1 ¼ of a cup of vegan flour
- ½ of a tsp of ground cardamom
- ½ of a tsp of baking soda
- ½ of a tsp of baking powder

**Appliances Needed:**
Instant Pot
Bundt Insert

**Directions:**
Use about 1 tbsp of coconut oil to be able to grease the inside of the bundt pan and place it on top of the water inside of your Instant Pot. Mix the rest of the ingredients up starting with the dry ingredients first. Mix the wet ingredients together and add to the dry ingredients so that you can make sure that you are able to get it all mixed. Use a hand mixer to get rid of any of the clumps that are in the cake and pour the batter into the bundt pan that is already inside of your Instant Pot. Put the lid on top of the pot and make sure that it is secured. The vent should be closed so

that pressure can build up in the pot. Put it on the manual function and set it to cook for 35 minutes. When it is done, allow the pot to depressurize before you try to open it up. Be cautious taking the lid off. Allow the cake to cool down before taking out of the pan or trying to serve.

### Notes on the Recipe:

While this is technically a recipe for a holiday cake, you can use this cake at any point throughout the year. The ingredients are easy to obtain and are delicious year-round. For other flavors, you can use different ingredients. Try making one with coconut and citrusy flavors as a fun summer treat.

### Nutritional Information:

| Calories | Fat | Sodium | Carbohydrates | Fiber | Sugar |
|---|---|---|---|---|---|
| 225 | 6 | 82 | 43 | 14 | 10 |

There are many different options for the cake. If you choose to use different options, the nutritional values will change. Please also be aware that this is only for *one* slice. The cake should be cut into eight pieces to make sure that you are getting an accurate example of what the nutritional information will look like.

## Simply Applesauce

Level of Difficulty: 3
Preparation Time: 15 minutes
Serving Size: 5 pints

**You Will Need:**
- 3 bags (about 32) small apples of your choice
- 1 tsp of nutmeg
- 1 frozen tin can of apple juice concentrated
- 1 tsp of ginger
- 3 tsp of cinnamon

**Appliances Needed:**
Instant Pot
Immersion Blender
5 Glass Pint Jars, Sterilized

**Directions:**
Cut all of your apples into four pieces each. Make sure that they are all roughly the same size so that they will cook evenly. Put each of the pieces that you have cut up into the pressure cooker and pour the liquid from the concentrate over top of them. Add the spices and stir everything up so that it is combined. Make sure that it does not go above the top of the fill line on your Instant Pot. Tighten the lid, shut the vent and turn the cooker to High Pressure. Watch it and only allow it to get to high pressure so that you don't overcook. As soon as it is at high pressure, unplug it from the wall or turn it off to begin reducing the heat. The pressure will release even though it will take a few minutes. Take the lid off and use an immersion blender to make sure that all of the skins are blended with the rest of the applesauce.

Transfer the sauce into each of the pints sized glass jars and make sure that they are sterilized before you do so. You can then put the lids on top of the applesauce and put it in your pressure cooker. Fill with water and cook using the sauce function until it is done. This part will take a few hours.

**Notes on the Recipe:**

If you want to make applesauce that is more like a dessert, you can use sugar or an artificial sweetener to make the recipe even sweeter. You can do anything to the applesauce, including different fruits, once you have the basic recipe done. If you want to make apple butter out of the recipe, you can just add ½ of a cup of brown sugar to it and follow the directions the same.

**Nutritional Information:**

| Calories | Fat | Sodium | Carbohydrates | Fiber | Sugar |
|---|---|---|---|---|---|
| 128 | .5 | 4 | 33.8 | 5.6 | 25.8 |

Even though this is packed with sugar, it comes almost exclusively from the apples and the apple juice that are in it. If you add more sugar to it to make it a sweeter version of applesauce, you will increase both the calories and the sugar count. The recipe should make 5 pints and the serving sizes are for 1/8th of a pint, but you can use more or less than that.

## Berry Granola Crunch

Level of Difficulty: 1
Preparation Time: 15 minutes
Serving Size: 4

### You Will Need:
- 1 frozen bag of blueberries
- 1 frozen bag of strawberries
- 1 frozen bag of raspberries
- (or, 3 frozen bags of mixed berries)
- 1 full cup of granola cereal
- ½ of a cup of sugar or natural sweetener
- ½ of a cup of applesauce

### Appliances Needed:
Instant Pot

### Directions:
Do not thaw any of your berries out because they will get mushy much faster when you are trying to cook them in the Instant Pot. Add all of the ingredients that you have to the Instant Pot and mix very well so that everything comes together. It should be sticky and almost dough-like in consistency. When everything is thoroughly mixed up, close the vent of the lid and put the lid on the pot, locking it into place so that it does not come loose during the cooking process. Set the Instant Pot to manual and let it cook for 10 minutes. When the 10 minutes are up, turn the pot completely off so that it will start to release some of the pressure that it built up while it was cooking. Make sure that you wait until it is depressurized before you try to take the lid off because you could hurt yourself. When it is done, serve warm.

**Notes on the Recipe:**

There are many different variations that you can do with this recipe. You can add tropical fruit or your favorite mixed fruit to the dish. You can also eliminate the sugar or sweetener for something that has just a hint of sweetness. You can also use the square Instant Pot insert or even the bundt pan insert to make the recipe more like a traditional one that you would make in your oven. No matter how you decide to make the dessert in your Instant Pot, it will be tasty. Serve with vegan ice cream or something else that you like with your sweet treats (the cocogurt is a great option to mix with this crispy berry treat!)

**Nutritional Information:**

| Calories | Fat | Sodium | Carbohydrates | Fiber | Sugar |
|---|---|---|---|---|---|
| 203 | 6 | 228 | 28 | 8 | 33.2 |

The oats that are in it allow it to be nutritional while the berries provide a lot of vitamins to help you live your best life. This is great as a dessert, but it can also be served with a lunch, dinner, as a snack or for breakfast. The nutritional information will change depending on what you add to it or what you do differently depending on what you put into it and the way that you change the recipe so be sure to mark down any changes that you have made to the recipe.

# Salted Caramelly Chick Peas

Level of Difficulty: 1
Preparation Time: 15 minutes
Serving Size: 4

**You Will Need:**
- 2 tin cans of chick peas that have been drained and rinsed
- ¼ of a cup of coconut oil
- ¼ of a cup of brown sugar
- 1 tsp of sea salt

**Appliances Needed:**
Instant Pot
Stove

**Directions:**
Make sure that your chick peas do not have any of the sticky skins on the outside. Skin them if they do and throw away the hulls. Heat your coconut oil on your stove in a small sauce pan until it starts to bubble up. Pour your brown sugar in with the coconut oil and stir until it starts to thicken up and get a nice, smooth texture. It may take some time. As soon as it starts to bubble up again, take it off of the heat before it has the chance to burn. Place your chickpeas into the mixture and stir to coat them. You can, at this point, put them in the fridge overnight so that they take on the flavor of the caramel sauce, but you can also just put them right into the Instant Pot.

If you are going to cook them right away, add the sea salt on top of the caramel and the chickpeas. Mix it together and sprinkle with just a little more without mixing together.

Place the chickpeas into your Instant Pot and seal the lid so that it does not come undone while you are cooking your chick pea mixture. Make sure that it is on tight and that the vent is closed as much as possible. You can then set it on the manual setting and push the up arrow until it says 10. This is the 10 minute setting, and your chickpeas will be done in that time. When you take them out, they should be sticky and cluster-like. If you want them to be dried out, you can take your time and cook them for another 10 or 15 minutes. They should dry out and become very crunchy.

**Notes on the Recipe:**
Try adding different seasonings, like nutmeg to the mixture so that you are able to get different flavors out of the chickpeas. They are so versatile and so packed with fiber that they can make you feel full even if you are just eating them as a dessert. You can also experiment with different options and include different flavors in them that are savory *or* sweet so that you will be able to do more with what you have. They make a great snack.

**Nutritional Information:**

| Calories | Fat | Sodium | Carbohydrates | Fiber | Sugar |
|---|---|---|---|---|---|
| 406 | 12 | 1600 | 58 | 9.8 | 8 |

As you can see, this recipe is not great for everyday consumption. The coconut oil adds a lot of fat to it and can make it seem unhealthy. The carb and sodium count are also very high so save this one for a special treat or for special occasions only to keep yourself from indulging in it too much or from making yourself sick from all of the extra sweetness that you get. If you are using savory spices in it and no "caramel" sauce, the calorie count should go down.

# Mocha Oatmeal

Level of Difficulty: 1
Preparation Time: 12 minutes
Serving Size: 2

**You Will Need:**
- 1 full cup of oats
- 1 full cup of water
- 1 full cup of coffee (brewed)
- ¼ of a cup of sugar
- ¼ of a cup of dairy free dark chocolate

**Appliances Needed:**
Instant Pot

**Directions:**
Before you begin cooking this recipe, chop up the dark chocolate into small pieces or simply get the chocolate chips that are dairy free (which can be hard to find). You can mix all of the ingredients together so that the chocolate will become melty and the coffee flavor will become infused into the oatmeal. The sugar will give it just the right amount of sweetness, and you'll be able to make sure that you are getting the little kick of tasty coffee that you need after a meal. Add the ingredients to the Instant Pot and place the lid on making sure that it is sealed. Cook using the manual setting until it is done. The oatmeal will be hot so give it some time to cool off.

**Notes on the Recipe:**
You can use regular coffee or decaf depending on how much of a kick that you want your oatmeal to have. As with most of the dessert recipes, you can use this as a breakfast

recipe. The best part about doing it this way and eating it for breakfast is that you don't need to drink your coffee separately. It will already be in your oatmeal!

**Nutritional Information:**

| Calories | Fat | Sodium | Carbohydrates | Fiber | Sugar |
|---|---|---|---|---|---|
| 362 | 8.9 | 21 | 65 | 4.8 | 36.2 |

If you like your coffee black and you just want the flavor of coffee in your oatmeal, eliminate the sugar and the chocolate from the recipe. This will allow it to taste the way that you like and the number of calories will be drastically reduced. The carbohydrates will also be cut by about half of the number that is in there because it will come only from the oatmeal instead of the sugar that is added to it.

# Black Bean Brownies

Level of Difficulty: 3
Preparation Time: 20 minutes
Serving Size: 8

## You Will Need:
- 2 tin cans of black beans
- 1 tsp of baking soda
- 1 tsp of baking powder
- 1 banana
- 1 tsp of salt
- ¼ of a cup of natural vegan sweetener
- ¼ of a cup of coconut oil that has already been melted

## Appliances Needed:
Instant Pot
Food processor
Square pan for Instant Pot (optional)

## Directions:
Put both of the cans of black beans, liquid included, into your food processor. Blend them until they completely mixed up and there are no chunks of them that are left in the food processor. Make sure that they are still a dough like consistency and are not liquid form yet. Mix those and the rest of the ingredients together in a bowl and use a hand mixer to make sure that they are completely blended up. This should result in the mixture becoming more liquid than a solid. It should pour easily in the way that you would expect brownie batter to be able to pour. Place the square pan into your Instant Pot. If you do not have a square pan insert for your Instant Pot, it is acceptable to use just the bottom of the Instant Pot. Make sure that you

rub the pot or the pan down with coconut oil to grease the sides so that the brownie does not get stuck to it.

Pour your brownie batter into the pot or into the pan that is in the pot and make sure that it does not go over the side. If you are using a pan, you should have already put water down into the bottom of your Instant Pot. Put your lid on top of the Instant Pot and cook on the manual setting for 13 minutes or until the brownies are done. Similar to real brownies, a toothpick stuck through the center of the pan of brownies should come out with nothing on it. When they are done, let the pan cool down before you take them out of the pan. If you are using the square pan, cut them into a 4x2 pattern so that you have exactly eight of them.

**Notes on the Recipe:**

You can add walnuts to the top of these after they are done the cooking. You can also add other things into them like raspberries or even candy canes that are vegan. Make sure that you check whatever you are adding to the recipe to make sure that it is, in fact, vegan. You may be surprised that the things you thought were vegan are, in fact, not. Any things that you are going to add into the batter should be done before cooking. Anything that you wish to place on top of the brownies should be done after they have finished cooking.

**Nutritional Information:**

| Calories | Fat | Sodium | Carbohydrates | Fiber | Sugar |
|---|---|---|---|---|---|
| 458 | 8.4 | 455 | 76.2 | 16 | 10.3 |

To make these even sweeter, you can add sugar to them. Just be sure that you adjust the nutritional information if you add sugar. A sugar free sweetener will have far fewer calories and carbohydrates than adding actual sugar would but the sugar is great if you are looking for a super sweet treat or a pick-me-up.

# Conclusion

Thank you for making it through to the end of this book, let's hope it was informative and was able to provide you with all of the recipes that you need to be able to use with your Instant Pot. We hope that all vegans (and people who simply like to eat vegan food) will be able to get the most out of this cookbook. The recipes were put together with care and with your taste buds in mind. The flavors are varied, the recipes are easy, and the ingredients are so cheap for you to buy.

The next step is to get all of the ingredients and fire up your Instant Pot.

Finally, if you found this book useful in anyway, a review on Amazon is always appreciated!

# The China Diet Study Cookbook

*Plant-Based Whole Food Recipes for Every Taste!*

© Copyright 2016 by Gabriel Montana - All rights reserved.

The follow eBook is reproduced below with the goal of providing information that is as accurate and reliable as possible. Regardless, purchasing this eBook can be seen as consent to the fact that both the publisher and the author of this book are in no way experts on the topics discussed within and that any recommendations or suggestions that are made herein are for entertainment purposes only. Professionals should be consulted as needed prior to undertaking any of the action endorsed herein.

This declaration is deemed fair and valid by both the American Bar Association and the Committee of Publishers Association and is legally binding throughout the United States.

Furthermore, the transmission, duplication or reproduction of any of the following work including specific information will be considered an illegal act irrespective of if it is done electronically or in print. This extends to creating a secondary or tertiary copy of the work or a recorded copy and is only allowed with express written consent from the Publisher. All additional right reserved.

The information in the following pages is broadly considered to be a truthful and accurate account of facts and as such any inattention, use or misuse of the information in question by the reader will render any resulting actions solely under their purview. There are no scenarios in which the publisher or the original author of this work can be in any fashion deemed liable for any hardship or damages that may befall them after undertaking information described herein.

Additionally, the information in the following pages is intended only for informational purposes and should thus be thought of as universal. As befitting its nature, it is presented without assurance regarding its prolonged validity or interim quality. Trademarks that are mentioned are done without written consent and can in no way be considered an endorsement from the trademark holder.

# Table of Contents

Introduction ................................................................. 1

Chapter 1: So, what is the China Study Diet? ........................... 4

Chapter 2: Recipes for Breakfast ................................... 12

Chapter 3: Recipes for Lunch ....................................... 25

Chapter 4: Recipes for Dinner ...................................... 38

Chapter 5: Recipes for Your Sweet Tooth .......................... 52

Chapter 6: Soup Recipes to Warm Your Soul ....................... 60

Conclusion ................................................................ 68

# Introduction

Congratulations on downloading *The China Diet Study Cookbook: Plant-Based Whole Food Recipes for Every Taste!* And thank you for doing so.

Imagine a life where your waistline is the last thing on your mind. You're skinny, you feel good, and you look phenomenal. All of this is possible through the secrets that exist within this book, *The China Diet Study Cookbook: Plant-Based Whole Food Recipes for Every Taste!* This book contains proven secrets to living a longer, healthier and more prosperous life. If you've tried other diets in the past and have walked away feeling unfilled or as if you were right back at your starting weight months after discontinuing the diet, this book is for you. The basis of any successful diet is to implement changes that result in a lifestyle change. The change that you need and deserve can be easily found by purchasing this book. What more could you ask for?

Especially in America, the idea of leading a healthy and fit lifestyle can sometimes seem like a dream and nightmare all at the same time. On the one hand, there are multiple diets that you can try and are popular at any given point in time, but often these diets seem like a fad. What's more, sometimes these diets don't even work, and you end up right back where you started. The China study diet is different. After learning about the principles of the China study diet, you'll be given amazingly simple and delicious recipes that you can begin to integrate into your own life. What more could you ask for?

You are guaranteed to learn:

- What the China Study Diet is and how you can benefit from it

- How the China Study Diet can be exactly the lifestyle change that your life needs

- Countless easy and delicious recipes that will make your palate pop!

Most of us have heard online and in the news that people living in the Chinese culture tend to live longer than people living in the American culture. Most commonly, the primary reason contributed to this fact is diet choices. The Chinese culture is known for its plant-based, rice-rich diet, and this is something that simply is not valued in American culture. Instead, Americans indulge in big fatty cheeseburgers, sodas at every meal, and grumble when they have to get up from the couch to find the remote control. The following chapters will provide you with a comprehensive understanding of why you should start considering the China Study Diet. This book will provide you with recipes that you need to start making smarter dieting choices, choices that will cause you to live longer. Everyone wants to experience the most of what life has to offer. How are you supposed to do that as you progress into your later years of life if you are constantly limited by health and nutritional constraints? Nourish yourself now and avoid the hassle of sickness and immobility years later in life.

Even if you currently have a fast metabolism and feel as if you wouldn't benefit from a diet that completely eliminates meat sources, it's likely that there will come a day when your metabolism will slow, your youthful features will fade, and the need to reign in your diet will become apparent. If you start now, and develop healthy habits slowly over time, your body and mind will be better prepared for when changes begin to occur. I know what you're thinking, "I'll never get old." It's easy to convince yourself of that, but the day will come. In this way, the recipes presented in this book will help to prepare you for the future and guarantees to keep you healthy along the way until you get there.

There are plenty of books on this subject on the market, thanks again for choosing this one! Every effort was made to ensure it is full of as much useful information as possible, please enjoy!

# Chapter 1: So, what is the China Study Diet?

The China Study Diet became popular because of an unhealthily reality that was and still is facing the lives of hundreds of thousands American people. Today, over thirty-five percent of the American population is considered to be obese. While this obesity results in physically larger people and higher amounts of consumption as an entire population, there are also serious health risks that are associated with this type of behavior. Cancer rates, heart disease, diabetes and high blood pressure can all be associated with eating poorly over a long period of time. This isn't meant to scare you, it's simply a reality. These harsh realities prompted two men by the names of Thomas M. Campbell and T. Colin Campbell to publish the book *The China Study: The Most Comprehensive Study of Nutrition Ever Conducted and the Startling Implications for Diet, Weight Loss, and Long-Term Health*. The two men are son and father, respectively. Their book is backed by extensive research done in the Philippines and China, and by their educations in nutritional health and science. The crux of their book is the idea that eating food made from animals creates an internal bodily environment that is much more likely to contract a potentially deadly disease than if animals were avoided altogether.

Of course, the Campbells' book has sparked major controversy in the area of nutritional health; however, they have answers to all of the backlash that has resulted from their publication. For example, a major controversial aspect of their research is the idea of protein. It's often said that the American diet is great because it offers individuals a wide variety of protein sources. The authors of this study argue that while animal protein in small doses can be beneficial to the body, Americans eat way more protein than they need, which results in the diseases that were discussed above. Instead, the two authors suggest that the adoption of an entirely plant-based diet that relies primarily on vegetables will help to eliminate diseases and help to promote a longer life.

Their findings are not based simply on their own personal thoughts; rather, they spent time in over sixty towns and counties in China, conducting research and gaining insight on the nutritional health of people living there. What gave this type of research an advantage over research that's been done in the past on human nutrition is that they were able to actually conduct studies on humans instead of animals. This type of research is rare for this field, and it gives their findings more credibility than studies that were done on animals in the past. They chose to conduct questionnaires and blood tests on over six thousand Chinese citizens, and ultimately found huge negative correlations between lifestyles, diet, and disease variables. In other words, the healthier a person's lifestyle and diet, the lower the potential was that he or she was vulnerable to a life alternating and potential deadly disease.

The diseases that the China Study claims will less likely target you if you adopt the lifestyle change that's presented in the book include:

- Alzheimer's

- Diabetes
- Heart disease

- High cholesterol

- Kidney stones

- Liver cancer

- Lupus

- Obesity

- Prostate cancer

- Rectal cancer

This list is not exhaustive. There are other diseases that the China Study diet can eliminate, allegedly. By looking at this list, it's obvious to see why the China Study diet would be enticing to someone who is looking to both lose weight and start living in a healthier way. Now that you're aware of the reasons why millions of people have heard about what the China Study Diet has to offer and how it can help to reduce the risk for potential diseases, let's take a look at what foods are okay to eat while on the China Study Diet and what foods should be avoided.

## Foods to Avoid While on the China Study Diet

Foods that should be avoided while on the China Study Diet include the following:

**Meat:** Any and all meat including steak, chicken, pork, turkey, lamb etc.

**Eggs:** While eggs should be avoided altogether, anything with a high egg content should also be avoided. This includes cakes, mayonnaise, and certain types of cookies

**Dairy:** Any cheese, milk, or yogurt should be avoided while on this diet. This includes all products that contain dairy. Instead, this diet promotes the consumption of soy products, or almond milk.

# Foods to Consume in Small Amounts While on the China Study Diet

Instead of completely avoiding the list below, it's acceptable to consume these foods in small amounts when on the China Study Diet:

**Fish:** It's okay to consume fish, as long as it's lean. Salmon, tuna, cod, and flounder can be consumed in small amounts. To the best of your ability, try to make sure that this food is locally sourced and raised humanely. Bottom-eating sea creatures, such as shrimp, lobster, and crabs should not be included in the fish category and should be avoided while on the China Study Diet.

**Simple Carbohydrates:** Simple carbohydrates are broken down more quickly by the body than complex carbohydrates. Although it might sound like it's good that these types of carbohydrates breakdown quickly, it's actually bad because then they get converted into sugar and turn into fat. They also provide you with less energy over a long period of time than complex carbohydrates. If you've ever felt tired after consuming a sugary donut or after chugging a sugary drink, you have experienced the short-term energy burst that simple carbohydrates can provide you. This being the case, pasta and crackers that don't contain whole grain should be only consumed in small doses, as should white bread, pastries and cereal. It's often not realized, but even "healthy" cereal can contain high amounts of sugar that are actually bad for the body.

**Types of Oil:** The China Study diet suggests that pretty much all types of oil should be limited to small amounts of consumption. This includes olive oil, something that can seem hard to avoid. Because oils are fatty, they should only be used when cooking, and for not much else.

Now that you understand what not to eat, let's take a look at the nutritional, whole foods that you should be consuming while adhering to this type of diet.

## Foods to Consume to Your Heart's Content while on the China Study Diet

Here is a comprehensive list of the foods that you can eat while on the China Study Diet:

**Fruit:** Apples, apricots, avocados, bananas, blueberries, cherries, coconuts, cranberries, dates, figs, grapes, raisins, grapefruits, kiwi, lemons, limes, lychees, mangos, melons, cantaloupes, honeydew, watermelon, clementine's, mandarin oranges, tangerines, papaya, passionfruit, peaches, pears, plums, pineapples, pomegranates, raspberries, tomatoes, etc.

**Vegetables:** Artichokes, arugula, boy choy, broccoli, cabbage, carrots, cauliflower, celery, chard, collard greens, corn, fennel, kale, lettuce, mushrooms, spinach, okra, onion, chives, garlic, leeks, shallots, peppers, parsley, peppers, pimentos, jalapeno, radishes, beets, parsnip, turnips, acorn squash, butternut squash, cucumbers, pumpkin, jicama, potatoes, sweet potatoes, yams, taro, water chestnuts, zucchini, tomatoes, cauliflower, etc.

Note: While all of the items on the above list are indeed vegetables, mushrooms are considered to be a fungus. Additionally, tomatoes and cucumbers are formally considered fruit, but they are generally classified as vegetables. This being the case, they're on this list as vegetables instead of fruit.

**Legumes:** Alfalfa, bean sprouts, black beans, black-eyed peas, chickpeas, green beans, kidney beans, all types of lentils, lima beans, mung beans, pinto beans, split peas, soy beans, peas, etc.

**Seeds and nuts:** Almonds, cashews, hazelnut, macadamia nuts, peanuts, pecans, pine nuts, walnuts, flax seeds, sesame seeds, sunflower seeds, peanut butter, tahini, etc.

Notes: While peanuts are generally considered to be a type of nut, they are technically a legume.

**Whole Grains:** Barley, buckwheat, corn, millet, any type of oats, quinoa, rye, brown rice, spelt, bulgur wheat, oat flour, spelt flour, whole grain flour, whole wheat couscous, rice pasta, whole grain wheat pasta, whole grain tortillas, whole grain buns, breadcrumbs, wheat germ, baked tortilla chips, etc.

**Beverages:** Water. Anything processed should mostly be avoided, and most beverages other than water are processed.

**Condiments and Spices:** Balsamic vinegar, regular vinegar, vegetable broth, salsa that contains low amounts of salt, chili paste, sea salt, soy sauce that contains little salt, pickles, mustard, miso, marinara sauce, tamari, apple cider vinegar, etc.

**Herbs and Spices:** Red pepper flakes, paprika, poppy seeds, onion powder, Old Bay seasoning, nutmeg, curry powder, rosemary, oregano, thyme, dill, mint, basil, cilantro, celery seeds, black pepper, coriander, Italian seasoning, ginger, etc.

**Dairy Substitutes:** Soy milk, almond milk, rice milk, soy yogurt, etc.

**Sweeteners:** Raw sugar, stevia, dried fruits like raisins and dates, agave syrup, molasses, jams, brown rice syrup, pureed fruits like bananas and applesauce, orange juice, etc.

While it would have been easier to simply state that you should be eating fruits, vegetables, and whole foods while on the China Study Diet, seeing all of the foods that you are allowed to eat while on the diet can help to make the diet more tangible and real. While there are certainly limitations to this type of diet, there are also a wide range of fruits, vegetables, whole grains, dairy substitutes and sweeteners that you can cook with and consume instead of meat, poultry, and fish.

## Veganism, Vegetarianism, and the China Study Diet

It's important to understand that the authors of the original China Study Diet book are not interested in associating their diet with the vegan or vegetarian lifestyle. The key difference, at least for the authors, is the idea that vegan and vegetarian are backed by ideological motivations. These ideals include the desire to minimize animal cruelty, and the desire to take a stand against the powers of big farming and government subsidies. Instead of wishing to eliminate this type of injustice from the world, China Study authors were mostly concerned with finding out empirical evidence about nutrition on the body. Their conclusions led them to believe that the type of lifestyle that best promotes the longevity of life and overall health is one that involves no meat or dairy consumption, separate from any idealistic overarching goals.

## A Few Notes About the Remainder of this Book

Now that you have a comprehensive understanding of what the China Diet is and what foods are allowed to be consumed within its parameters, the rest of this book will give you valuable recipes that you can easily use to make the transition to this new way of life easier and fun. In addition to the recipes, tips will also be provided on how you can take a specific recipe from good to great in terms of the quality of the food that you've purchased. Each chapter will start with the easiest recipes, and progress towards recipes that are slightly more difficult and or time consuming.

# Chapter 2: Recipes for Breakfast

Breakfast, after all, is the most important meal of the day. This chapter will document recipes that are sure to brighten your morning and make the rest of your day a great one.

## Breakfast Recipe 1: Avocado and Refried Beans on Toast

Level of Difficulty: 1

Preparation Time: 5 Minutes

Serving Size: 2 Bread Slices

### You Will Need:

- 1 avocado, sliced into thin strips
- 2 whole grain sandwich slices
- 1 cup of vegan refried beans
- Coarse sea salt to taste
- *Optional:* a couple of slices of white raw onion

### Appliances Needed:
- 1 toaster

## Directions

Begin by picking out two slices of bread from the loaf that you have. Place these two slices of bread into your toaster and toast them to your personal desired level of crispiness. If you are making a slice for a friend or a family member, make sure that you know ahead of time how crispy they want their toast too. While the bread is toasting, put the refried beans on either the stove or the microwave and cook until creamy and rich. You should be able to easily stir with a fork. While the refried beans are cooking, slice the avocado to meet your preferences. When the toast jumps up from the toaster and the refried beans are ready, generously dollop the refried beans onto the toast and spread generously over the toast with either a fork or a knife. Place the avocado on top. If you've decided to include white onion, garnish on top of the avocado and season with salt. Serve right away, as the avocado will brown if it sits out for too long.

## Notes for this Recipe:

- It's important to make sure that you purchase vegan refried beans before using them in this recipe. Many people are unaware of this, but refried beans that are prepared at a restaurant are rarely vegetarian because they usually contain animal lard.

## Nutritional Information:

This nutritional information is for one slice of refried beans with avocado:

| Calories | Fat | Sodium | Carbohydrates | Fiber | Sugar |
|---|---|---|---|---|---|
| 484 | 13 grams | 1,272 milligrams | 56 grams | 27 grams | 2 grams |

While four-hundred and eighty-four calories may seem like a lot for breakfast, let's take a moment to think about where the majority of these calories are coming from. The primary source of calories within this breakfast is the avocado. Coming in at 240 calories per avocado, it comprises roughly half of the overall calories for this morning meal. Besides the calories, the other striking aspect of this nutritional chart is the sodium, which can be contributed to the refried beans. It might be worth your while to look for low-sodium refried beans so that you can eliminate the rather high sodium levels that this breakfast option offers. You can also opt to make the refried beans yourself instead of purchasing ones in a can. Overall, this extremely easy recipe is sure to make your taste buds say, "Wow!"

# Breakfast Recipe 2: Granola with Peanut Butter and Bananas

Level of Difficulty: 1

Preparation Time: 20 minutes

Serving Size: 2 bowlfuls

## You Will Need:

- 2 tablespoons peanut butter
- 2 tablespoons honey
- 1 cup of whole rolled oats
- ¼ teaspoon of vanilla
- ¼ teaspoon of cinnamon

## Appliances Needed:

- A conventional oven

## Directions

Begin this recipe by preheating your oven to 325 degrees Fahrenheit. Quickly take a moment to spray a cookie sheet with non-stick cooking spray, at set the sheet off to the side for the time being. Next, you'll want to combine your equal parts peanut butter and honey into a bowl, and microwave this combination until the peanut butter melts. This should take about thirty seconds. Next, take this out of the microwave and stir until both are combined nicely. Stir in the cinnamon and vanilla, and then finally add the oats. Stir the oats until they are adequately coated with the honey and peanut butter mixture. Then, spread the oat mixture onto the cookie sheet that's been waiting to be used. Bake the oats in the oven for between six to eight minutes. You should be watching for the oats to appear golden brown. When golden, remove from oven and set to cool.

## Notes for this Recipe:

- While the China Study Diet does not explicitly discuss whether or not honey should be included or exclude from the China Study Diet, you can use agave nectar or brown rice syrup, both which are approved by the diet guidelines.

## Nutritional Information:

This nutritional information is for one entire cup of the peanut butter oat blend.

| Calories | Fat | Sodium | Carbohydrates | Fiber | Sugar |
|---|---|---|---|---|---|
| 628 | 23 grams | 8 milligrams | 104 grams | 12 grams | 38 grams |

The nutritional information provided for this recipe proves that this breakfast choice might be best reserved for occasional usage, rather than every day consumption. While 628 calories will certainly tide you over until lunch time, the amount of sugar and carbohydrates in this recipe suggest that this recipe is best consumed in moderation. Of course, while the sodium levels are low compared to the avocado recipe that was previously discussed, the levels of sugar are much higher.

# Breakfast Recipe 3: Pecan and Cinnamon Quinoa

Level of Difficulty: 2

Preparation Time: 25 minutes

Serving Size: 4

## You Will Need:

- 4 teaspoons agave nectar
- ¼ cup chopped pecans
- ½ teaspoon ground cinnamon
- 2 ½ cups blackberries, preferably fresh
- 1 cup quinoa
- 1 cup water
- 1 cup milk (Obviously, milk that doesn't come from an animal)

## Appliances Needed:

- Conventional oven
- Skillet
- Saucepan

## Directions

First, preheat your oven to 350 degrees Fahrenheit. While the oven is preheating, fill your saucepan with the water, the quinoa, and the milk. The heat under the saucepan should be on high, so that the mixture can be brought to a boil. Once the mixture is boiling, reduce the heat to a low or medium temperature and cover with a lid. Let this simmer for about 15 minutes, or until most of the liquid has been absorbed by the heat. As you're waiting for the quinoa to finish cooking, coat the skillet with non-stick cooking spray and toast the pecans for roughly one and a half minutes on each side. Turn off the heat, and let the mixture cool for about five minutes. Next, add the cinnamon and the blackberries, and serve at your leisure. Then add the pecans to the top of the quinoa mixture. Don't forget to drizzle the agave nectar on top of each serving of your delicious and simple breakfast!

## Notes for this Recipe:

- You can consider this recipe to be similar to cooking rice. Just like rice, quinoa can absorb any liquid that is cooking with it at the same time. If you have a rice cooker, this recipe can go from being one that needs to be monitored to one that requires very little attention.

- The reason that this recipe is described as a level of difficulty of two instead of one is because of the pecans. If you're not careful when toasting the pecans, it's likely that you will burn the pecans easily and cause a mess for yourself. Make sure that the pecans are cooked on low heat, and be patient while they cook. Otherwise, it's likely that you could set off your fire alarm (take it from someone who knows from experience!)

- Don't be afraid to experiment with this recipe. If blackberries aren't your first fruit of choice, maybe try blueberries or raspberries instead. Additionally, if you're not interested in eating pecans, walnuts are a great substitute.

- Any type of quinoa can be used for this recipe. Also, if you're not used to cooking with quinoa, don't be afraid to try it. Quinoa has a ton of nutritional benefits, including large amounts of protein and iron.

## Nutritional Information:

This nutritional information is for one fourth cup serving of quinoa.

| Calories | Fat | Sodium | Carbohydrates | Fiber | Sugar |
|---|---|---|---|---|---|
| 448 | 15.5 | 195 milligrams | 172 grams | 25 grams | 14 grams |

While the nutritional information for this recipe may seem relatively harmless, it's important to note here that consuming quinoa in large amounts often leads to weight gain. This is due to the fact that quinoa consists of a lot of calories, in addition to a large number of carbohydrates. Keep this in mind as you begin to move towards the China Study Diet. Quinoa, while it can be especially delicious when combined with fruit, should be eaten in moderation, just like most foods should be.

# Breakfast Recipe 4: Chickpea Crepe with Filling

Level of Difficulty: 3

Preparation Time: 10 minutes

Serving Size: 1 large pancake

## You Will Need:

- ½ cup of chickpea flour
- 1 scallion stalk, roughly chopped
- ¼ cup red pepper
- ¼ teaspoon garlic powder
- ¼ teaspoon baking powder
- ¼ teaspoon sea salt
- 1/8 teaspoon black pepper
- 2 ½ tablespoons water
- *Optional:* Red pepper flakes to taste
- *For serving purposes:* salsa, avocado, hummus

## Appliances Needed:

- A large skillet

## Directions

Begin by heating your large skillet over medium-high heat. As your skillet is preheating, find a medium-sized bowl and whisk together your chickpea flour, salt, pepper, garlic powder, baking powder, and red pepper flakes (if you are using them). Then, add your water and whisk that into the mixture. This mixture should be smooth, with no clumps or blemishes remaining. For me, this usually means that I whisk this mixture for about thirty seconds, to ensure that there are plenty of air bubbles in the mixture. Next, pour in all of your cut-up vegetables. At this point, it's safe to say that your skillet will be plenty heated and ready to go. To make sure, you can pour a drop of water into the skillet and see that it sizzles. Then, *liberally* coat the skillet with either olive oil or non-stick cooking spray, and pour all of the batter into the skillet. Cook batter on each side of the crepe for between five to six minutes, until you can easily flip the crepe with a fork or a spatula. Serve with the suggesting toppings, and add any toppings that you see fit. Enjoy!

## Notes for this Recipe:

- If instead of buying chickpea flour, you'd prefer to make your own, simply use a food processor or a blender to mash up the chickpeas until they are fine and flour-like consistency.

- It's important to realize that while this crepe looks almost like a pancake, it can take a lot longer to cook than the traditional disc-like breakfast treat. Have patience, and make sure that you cook the crepe long enough so that its insides are not mushy.

- The chickpea flour has a tendency to stick to the skillet. Make sure to spray your skillet liberally! If not, you'll end up with a crepe that has half of its body missing.

## Nutritional Information:

This nutritional information is for one crepe.

| Calories | Fat | Sodium | Carbohydrates | Fiber | Sugar |
|---|---|---|---|---|---|
| 250 | 8 grams | 60 milligrams | 60 grams | 12 grams | 15 grams |

Even though this recipe takes the most work in terms of prepping the vegetables and making the flour (if you choose to make your own flour), it's one of the healthier breakfast options that we've discussed within this chapter. While quinoa is considered healthier than a chick pea because quinoa is considered to be a complete protein, all you need to do is simply combine this breakfast option with a whole grain in order to make the dish one that provides the benefits of consuming a complete protein. Of course, from the calories that are found in one large crepe, it might be a good idea to consumer two of these for breakfast instead of one so that you're not hungry before lunchtime; however, due to the filling and hearty quality of this recipe, you might find that you're less hungry than you think after eating it.

It's important to remember upon diving into the China Study Diet that you should be making these recipes specific to your preferences and dietary needs. The only way that this type of lifestyle change is going to work is if you are eating foods that you like and are being prepared in a way that makes you excited to eat. This being said, it's equally important to understand that you should be looking to leave your comfort zone a bit while experimenting with this diet. Try new foods, expand your palate, and don't look back as you move further from the foods that you have been used to eating in the past and foods that you will be eating on this new diet venture.

# Chapter 3: Recipes for Lunch

While breakfast might be considered the most important meal of the day, lunch can be considered the underrated MVP of the food world. The recipes presented in this chapter are sure to make your work friends jealous in both their simplicity and nutritional value. Stick with what this chapter has to offer and they'll be asking for your recipe secrets in no time.

## Lunch Recipe 1: Hummus Sandwich with Hearty Vegetables

Level of Difficulty: 1

Preparation Time: 10 minutes

Serving Size: 1 normal-sized sandwich

### You Will Need:

- 2 tablespoons of hummus
- 3 slices of cucumber, sliced to your desired level of thinness
- 2 slices of whole grain bread
- 2 slices of tomato, sliced to your desired level of thinness
- ¼ cup of thinly grated carrots
- ¼ cup sprouts of alfalfa

## Appliances Needed:

- 1 toaster

## Directions

Place the two slices of bread in the toaster and toast until they are crispy enough and to your liking. Once the bread is ready, take the teaspoons of the hummus and dollop one tablespoon each onto both slices of bread. Spread hummus onto sandwich bread pieces liberally. Next, layer the vegetables onto the sandwich in a way that makes sense to you. Finally, cut the bread into a pattern that makes you smile. Put the sandwich into either a lunchbox, paper bag, or Tupperware container and take to work. Enjoy later while your coworkers give you jealous looks.

## Notes for this Recipe:

- You want to make sure that you toast the bread for this recipe. Especially if you're making this sandwich early in the morning and then taking it with you to enjoy later in the day, the toasting will help to keep the sandwich durable. The last thing you want is a soggy hummus sandwich.

- Toothpicks can really help to keep this sandwich together, especially if it's being transported. It might be a good idea to buy some and stick them into your sandwich before packing it up and heading out for the day.

- While alfalfa sprouts are recommended for this recipe because they are rather thin and small in terms of greens, if you'd like an added crunch to your lunch you could also try using lettuce instead of alfalfa sprouts. While they're slightly less nutritional, lettuce could also make you feel like you're back to your old ways, munching on a subway sandwich on your much-needed lunch break.

- In addition to the alfalfa sprouts and the carrots that this recipe calls for, a great addition to this sandwich that will certainly complement the hummus would be red peppers.

## Nutritional Information:

This nutritional information is for one entire sandwich.

| Calories | Fat | Sodium | Carbohydrates | Fiber | Sugar |
|---|---|---|---|---|---|
| 336 | 12.8 grams | 291 milligrams | 44.5 grams | 12.5 grams | 5.3 grams |

In terms of lunch, this sandwich appears to be pretty low in calories. There's a chance that it will not be able to get you through the rest of your workday without evoking hunger or the need for a snack. To supplement this sandwich and avoid the need to chew off your arm while at work, you could bring fruit with this sandwich, or make yourself a smoothie.

# Lunch Recipe 2: Black Beans, Kale, and Avocado Burrito

Level of Difficulty: 1

Preparation Time: 10 minutes
Serving Size: 1 burrito

## You Will Need:

- 2 leaves of kale, washed thoroughly and cut into bite-sized chunks

- ½ of an avocado, a small avocado

- ½ black beans, drained and rinsed

- 1 tablespoon of fresh cilantro, chopped

- ½ teaspoon fresh jalapeno

- 1 garlic clove

- 1 tablespoon chopped red onion

- 1 eight-inch whole wheat tortilla

- *To Taste:* fresh lime juice

- *To Taste:* olive oil

- *To Taste:* cumin powder

- *To Taste:* chili powder

- *To Taste:* sea salt

## Appliances Needed:

- A skillet or a microwave, whichever you prefer

## Directions

To begin with this recipe, place the chopped kale into a bowl and marinate with the sea salt, the chili powder, the cumin, the olive oil, the lime juice, the jalapeno, and cilantro. Set aside for the time being. Next, turn your attention to the black beans. Combine them with the minced garlic and place them in a few tablespoons of water. Place the black beans and the garlic in either a skillet or the microwave with the water, and heat on a low-to-medium level of heat. If you're using the skillet, be sure to first sauté the garlic in olive oil before placing the beans in the skillet. Once the beans are warm and heated in their entirety, remove them from the heat source and mash the beans into a chunky blend. Set to the side for the time being.

After you're done preparing the beans, take your tortilla and place it either in the microwave or onto a fresh skillet so that the bottom of the tortilla remains clean. Once warm, remove the tortilla from the skillet and put onto a plate. Dollop the black bean mixture onto the tortilla first, and then add the avocado and kale. Lastly, add the red onion as a garnish. Cut the tortilla in half and consume while still warm.

## Notes for this Recipe:

- It's likely that you will have substantial amounts of kale leftover from this recipe. If this is the case, consider using this leftover kale as either a tasty side dish, or saving it and using it as a salad for a different meal later on in the week.

## Nutritional Information:

This is the nutritional information for one avocado, kale, and black bean tortilla wrap.

| Calories | Fat | Sodium | Carbohydrates | Fiber | Sugar |
|---|---|---|---|---|---|
| 600 | 6 grams | 800 milligrams | 60 grams | 10 grams | 3 grams |

While it may seem like this lunch dish contains a lot of calories, it's important to note that the majority of the calories in this recipe come from the whole-wheat tortilla wrap. Additionally, two grams of the sugar in this recipe also are a product of the tortilla wrap. If you were to remove the tortilla wrap and simply eat the black beans, the avocado, and the kale as a mixture on its own, you could cut down on the calories and sugar; however, the wrap is also providing the body with carbohydrates that it needs in order to function throughout the day.

# Lunch Recipe 3: Cherry, Kale, and Sunflower Seed Salad

Level of Difficulty: 2

Preparation Time: 20 minutes

Serving Size: Serves 4

## You Will Need:

- 2 tablespoons of sunflower seeds
- 5 ounces of baby kale
- ¼ cup dried cherries (not the cherries that are in a Shirley Temple)
- ¼ cup red onion, neatly sliced
- *For the Dressing:* 1 ½ tablespoons cider vinegar
- *For the Dressing:* 1 tablespoon olive oil
- *For the Dressing:* 1 teaspoon Dijon mustard
- *For the Dressing:* 1 teaspoon honey
- *For the Dressing:* ¼ teaspoon sea salt
- *For the Dressing:* ¼ teaspoon pepper

## Appliances Needed:

- You have the option of using a blender to combine the dressing ingredients. If you don't have a blender, a simple spoon, a medium sized bowl will do.

## Directions

Begin this recipe by first combining the ingredients for the dressing. Combine the apple cider vinegar, the olive oil, the Dijon mustard, the honey, the salt and the pepper into a large bowl. Either blend this mixture by hand or use the blender that you have at your disposal. Once this mixture is creamily blended and tastes delicious, pour over the cherries, the red onion, the sunflower seeds and the kale. Toss to evenly coat the entire mixture, and devour chilled.

## Notes for this Recipe:

- While you can certainly buy your dressing at the store, dressing bought at the store usually contains ingredients that are unhealthy for the body or contain a
- Large number of preservatives. This being the case, it's suggested that you make your own dressing instead of purchase it at the store. Doing this will ensure that you are completely aware of the ingredients that you're consuming and you'll be better able to adhere to the guidelines presented by the China Study Diet.

## Nutritional Information:

| Calories | Fat | Sodium | Carbohydrates | Fiber | Sugar |
|---|---|---|---|---|---|
| 400 | 6 grams | 300 milligrams | 66 grams | 30 grams | 36 grams |

The kale in this salad presents the ability to consume a vegetable with a wide variety of attributes. These include high fiber, high amounts of iron, high levels of vitamin K and high levels of vitamin A. Kale is also a great source of antioxidants. The cherries in this recipe are what cause certain aspects of this particular nutritional chart to be large. When you consider the fact that this salad will create a nice blend between pepperiness and sweetness for the palate, it makes it more reasonable to consume. Additionally, because the cherries are a natural source of sugar and carbohydrates, they will be digested differently in the body than say a can of soda or a sugary cake would be. For these reasons, this salad is considered to be a healthily and secure option for the aspiring China Study Diet enthusiast.

# Lunch Recipe 4: Sweet Potato Stuffed with Quinoa

Level of Difficulty: 3

Preparation Time: 1 hour and fifteen minutes

Serving Size: 4

## You Will Need:

- 4 medium sized sweet potatoes
- ¾ cup quinoa (any type of quinoa will do)
- 1 ¼ cup of water
- ¼ tablespoon cumin
- ¼ tablespoon sea salt
- ½ the juice of a lime
- ¼ cup sliced and diced red onion
- ¼ cup salsa
- *Optional: crushed up tortilla chips*
- *Optional: toasted pumpkin seeds*

## Appliances Needed:

- Conventional oven

- Food Processor

## Directions

Begin by preheating your oven to 400 degrees Fahrenheit. As the oven is preheating, make sure to poke a few holes into all four of your potatoes to ensure that they will cook through in their entirety. Set the potatoes aside for the time being. Once the oven has been successfully preheated, place the poked potatoes directly in the center of the oven rack and cook for roughly one hour. Be sure to check on the potatoes periodically to make sure that they are cooking evenly. Next, heat a small to medium sized saucepan on medium to high heat. Once hot and ready to go, add the quinoa to the saucepan and lightly toast for between three to five minutes. The quinoa should be only slightly toasted at this point. This step should ensure that the quinoa is completely dry before the cooking process begins. Next, add the water to the saucepan, a bit of sea salt, and lime juice. Bring these ingredients to a simmer in the pan, and then reduce this to low heat. Cook the quinoa for twenty minutes, so that it can absorb all of the lime juice, sea salt, and water. Once the quinoa has finished cooking, add the cumin to the quinoa and also add another large pinch of sea salt. Stir these seasonings into the quinoa, and add any flavor that the quinoa needs as you go.

To add the dressing for the sweet potatoes, blend together the rest of the ingredients, excluding the water, into a food processor, and pulp into a nice and creamy dressing. *Please Note:* You may need to add water at this point into the blender, but only enough water so that the ingredients can blend more easily. Be sure to taste the dressing and adjust the recipe as needed. Set the dressing aside for the moment, and prepare any of the toppings that you'd like to add to the potatoes, such as cilantro, chopped onions, or crushed tortilla chips. In order to prepare the potatoes to be stuffed, cut open the centers of each potato and press into the sides of each one to allow room for the quinoa, salsa, and other accoutrements. Once the quinoa has been added, don't forget to add the dressing on top and any of the toppings that you've opted for. Let it cool, and enjoy!

## Notes for this Recipe:

- Since the China Study Diet does not allow for many protein sources, you're going to have to get creative in how to supplement your protein intake. It's safe to say that by now you may have noticed that one way to do this is through a high intake of whole grains, such as quinoa. However, if you decide that you do not enjoy quinoa, a great substitute for this dish is black beans. Black beans will provide this potato with even more of the southwestern flavor that it deserves.

- When cooking the dressing for the potato, be sure to continuously scrape down the sides of the blender or the food processor as you go. Otherwise, you'll end up with more of a chunky salsa and less of a creamy, delicious dressing.

- Please also be aware that the nutritional information for this recipe allows for all of the ingredients except for the pumpkins seeds or the tortilla chips.

## Nutritional Information:

This nutritional information is for one sweet potato.

| Calories | Fat | Sodium | Carbohydrates | Fiber | Sugar |
|---|---|---|---|---|---|
| 504 | 15.8 grams | 307 milligrams | 84.8 grams | 14 grams | 5.2 grams |

Nutritionally, this sweet potato appears to be extremely healthy in quality. While it may take quite some time to cook, the good news about this recipe is that if you're in a rush you can certainly cook the sweet potatoes ahead of time and set them in the refrigerator. When you're ready to eat one, all you would have to do is stick the sweet potato in the oven and pour some of the dressing that you've preserved over the sweet potato when it's hot. This way, you can easily assemble the potato piecemeal while you're at work without any hassle. Additionally, you can sprinkle different toppings each day onto the potato, so that you can eat basically the same thing for lunch for a week without feeling bored or feeling like you're missing out on the pizza that your coworker is unhealthily enjoying.

# Chapter 4: Recipes for Dinner

While breakfast can be considered the most important meal of the day and lunch can be considered that awkward meal between breakfast and dinner, dinner is the staple meal that brings comfort and community to the home after a long day of work. Let's take a look at some of the recipes that will enhance your dieting experience for the better.

## Dinner Recipe 1: Portobello Pizza!

Level of Difficulty: 1

Preparation Time: 30 minutes

Serving Size: Between 2 to 3, depending on how hungry you are

### You Will Need:

- 3 Portobello mushrooms, the larger the better. They should be cleaned thoroughly with the stems removed

- ¼ teaspoon oregano, dried

- ¼ teaspoon basil, dried

- ¼ teaspoon garlic powder

- 1 cup pizza sauce

- ½ cup miscellaneous mixed vegetables. These should include any vegetables that you enjoy eating on a pizza.

- Olive oil to use as-needed

- *Optional:* Red pepper flakes

- *Optional:* Fresh basil

## Appliances Needed:

- A conventional oven

## Directions

Start this recipe by preheating your oven to 400 hundred degrees. Next, place your handsome Portobello mushrooms on a baking sheet and spread some olive oil on each side of the mushroom. Forgetting this step will lead to mushrooms sticking to your pan. You want to make sure that the mushrooms are both adequately coated but not oversaturated. After you've applied the olive oil, sprinkle the mushrooms with garlic powder, oregano and basil. Once your oven has preheated, bake these bad boys for five minutes.

As your mushrooms are prepping in the oven, cut up the vegetables that you've chosen to throw on your mini pizzas and prepare the pizza sauce that you're going to be using. Once the five minutes is up and the Portobello mushrooms have finished pre-baking, take them out of the oven and top them with the desired levels of pizza sauce and vegetables. Then bake in the oven for between fifteen to twenty minutes, or until the vegetables are fully cooked through.

## Notes for this Recipe:

- Due to the fact that most vegan cheeses are made of soy, it might be possible for you to find a vegan cheese that can complement this easy dinner nicely. Due to the fact that there can be many complicated ingredients in these types of cheeses, I left them out of this particular recipe so that calculating the nutritional information would be easier.

## Nutritional Information:

This nutritional information is for one Portobello pizza.

| Calories | Fat | Sodium | Carbohydrates | Fiber | Sugar |
|---|---|---|---|---|---|
| 165 | 10 grams | 627 milligrams | 14.5 grams | 4 grams | 5 grams |

This recipe certainly takes away any and all guilt that's associated with consuming a lot of pizza. This quick and easy meal has it all; protein, carbohydrates, and is low in calories. The only thing that you should watch out for with this recipe is the sodium levels. Be mindful of this, especially if you are considering adding vegan cheese to this recipe.

# Dinner Recipe 2: Hummus Wraps Made with Rainbow Chard

Level of Difficulty: 1

Preparation Time: 5 minutes

Serving Size: 1

## You Will Need:

- 1 leaf of the rainbow chard variety

- ¼ cup of hummus

- Vegetables to stick inside of the chard, such as cucumbers, peppers, onions, or tomatoes

## Appliances Needed:

- None

## Directions

Thoroughly wash and dry off your chard, making sure that it has been thoroughly cleaned. Next, pick out a nice leaf that is big and looks like it's up to the task of holding a large variety of vegetables within its green bosom. After you've found a leaf that's up to the task, set it aside and begin cutting your vegetables in a way that will complement the leaf that you've chosen. This might mean cutting large stalks of cucumbers so that the entire length of the rainbow chard leaf is encompassing it, or dicing the tomatoes in a way that ensures they won't be able to leave the chard nest. Be creative in this type of implementation. Once you have the vegetables the way that you like them, the next step is to spread your hummus over the chard leaf and place the vegetables on top of it. Wrap it up, and enjoy.

## Notes for this Recipe:

- In terms of simplicity, this might be the rawest and simplest meal that has been presented in this book thus far. Of course, you might not want to enjoy this meal at a formal sit down dinner with friends and family, but this is the perfect meal for an evening where you have somewhere to be and need a quick fix fast.

- Consider securing your wrap with toothpicks or cellophane, as this will keep the wrap fully in tact if you want to bring it with you on-the-go.

- You are welcome to substitute the rainbow chard for kale or collard greens, but be forewarned that this alteration will likely result in the wrap having a more bitter taste to it.

## Nutritional Information:

This nutritional information is for one rainbow chard vegetable wrap.

| Calories | Fat | Sodium | Carbohydrates | Fiber | Sugar |
|---|---|---|---|---|---|
| 123 | 6 grams | 0 grams | 13 grams | 5 grams | 2 grams |

    Because this is such a light meal, you might want to consider making a few of these for dinner, especially if you have a long night ahead of you. You could also make side dishes for yourself, such as sweet potatoes or rice.

# Dinner Recipe 3: The Perfect Shepherd's Pie

Level of Difficulty: 2

Preparation Time: 1 Hour

Serving Size: Serves 6

## You Will Need:

- 3 pounds Yukon Gold potatoes
- Salt and pepper to taste
- 1 medium onion
- 2 cloves of minced garlic
- 1 ½ cup of washed and uncooked lentils
- 4 cups of vegetable stock
- 2 teaspoons fresh thyme
- 1 bag of frozen mixed vegetables, a 10-ounce bag

## Appliances Needed:

- A conventional oven

# Directions

Preheat your oven to 425 degrees Fahrenheit. Spray a 9 x 13-inch pan with non-stick cooking spray, and set aside for the time being. Next, fill a large pot with water and place the potatoes into the water until they're just covered with it. You don't want the potatoes submerged too deeply. Bring this pot to a low boil on medium to high heat, generously salt these potatoes, and cook them for between twenty to thirty minutes. You'll know that they're done when the potatoes can be easily sliced with a knife without much effort. Once the potatoes have cooked, drain them so that there is no water remaining, and mash them until they're smooth and silky. Once they are mashed exactly the way that you enjoy your potatoes, season with salt and pepper to taste. You can set the potatoes aside once they've been cooked and are waiting to be baked.

Next, you'll want to sauté your onions and garlic in a saucepan or on a skillet for roughly five minutes. You want the onions to become translucent and the garlic to be slightly browned. Remember to cook the onion and the garlic in an adequate amount of olive oil. Once the garlic and the onions are mostly cooked, add the frozen vegetables to this mixture and add some salt and pepper as well. As the vegetables are cooking, make sure that the mixture tastes good to you. Add spice to this combination as needed. Once it tastes delicious, pour the skillet or saucepan into your 9 x 13-inch baking pan and top with the potatoes that have been waiting to be used. Smooth the potatoes down with a fork. You'll want to allow the Shepherd's pie to cook for ten to fifteen minutes, or until the mashed potatoes look golden on top. Unlike many of the other dishes that we've discussed in this book, you'll want to allow this dish to cool prior to serving it.

## Notes for this Recipe:

- Please note that this recipe will not fit in an 8 x 8-inch pan. It will, however, fit into a two-quart baking pan.

- You can use vegan butter in this recipe for the potatoes; however, this book does not necessarily recommend the use of faux-vegan products in its recipes.

- You can use arrowroot powder and add it to the vegetable mixture in order to thicken its contents and create a heartier feel for the overall dish. If you do this, there's a chance that it will more closely resemble the lamb dish that you're more accustomed to eating.

## Nutritional Information:

This nutritional information accounts for one sixth of the overall recipe.

| Calories | Fat | Sodium | Carbohydrates | Fiber | Sugar |
|---|---|---|---|---|---|
| 396 | 5.3 grams | 109 milligrams | 72 grams | 19 grams | 4 grams |

The nutritional information presented above demonstrates the fact that one serving of the Shepherd's pie may not be enough for one person. At 400 calories, an individual would have to make sure that he or she were eating more than 400 calories throughout the rest of the day in order to make up for the low caloric needs that this meal meets. Low in sugar and fat, the carbohydrates in this dish can be largely attributed to the

Yukon potatoes. This dish is the perfect meal to serve to a family that's in a hurry, because it can be made in advance and reheated quickly in the oven.

# Dinner Recipe 4: Falafel Burgers (Baked, not Fried)

Level of Difficulty: 3

Preparation Time: 1 hour

Serving Size: 4 patties

## You Will Need:

- ¼ - ½ cup gluten-free oat flour

- 3 cloves of garlic, large

- The juice of one large lemon

- ½ tablespoon of sea salt

- ½ tablespoon of pepper

- 1 ¼ teaspoon of cumin

- 1 fifteen-ounce can of chickpeas, thoroughly washed and drained

- *Optional:* Toppings such as tomatoes, onions or lettuce

- *Optional:* Turn this into a wrap by adding a whole-wheat pita

## Appliances Needed:

- Food processor or blender
- A skillet

## Directions

Begin by preheating your oven to 375 degrees Fahrenheit. Next, grab your food processor and begin mixing the following ingredients together: parsley, garlic, lemon juice, cumin, and a pinch of each the salt and the pepper. Blend all of these until they're well combined. Next, you'll want to add the chickpeas into the food processor, and blend them with the spices in a way so that they're still a little chunky when you're finished. There's no need to process the chickpeas into a pulp. Once you're satisfied with the texture of your chickpea blend, remove from the food processor or the blender and add the oat flour to it. Use your hands to knead the flour into the chickpeas so that it forms a dough. You'll want to adjust the flavor of the patty as you do this. Form the balls of dough into half-inch thick patties of falafel, and then refrigerate these patties for at least fifteen minutes. You really want the patties to firm so that they'll maintain their shape as they make their way to your plate. Once they've hardened, place the falafel patties onto a baking sheet so that they can bake for between thirty to forty minutes. At around the fifteen to twenty-minute mark, you'll want to flip the patties to ensure that they're cooking evenly on each side.

# Notes for this Recipe:

- Instead of using gluten-free oat flour for this recipe, you also have the option of using grounded almonds, pecans, or walnuts instead.

- Instead of baking your falafel, you can opt to fry your falafel in a skillet. To do this, add olive or canola oil to a skillet and turn the heat to a medium-high level. Once the pan has been adequately coated with olive oil, place the refrigerated falafel patty into the pan and cook on each side for between three to four minutes on each side. Once they've been fried, they will still need to bake. Place them back into the oven on the baking sheet and cook as directed normally.

- Be advised that the longer you cook the falafel patties, the firmer they'll get. While this may seem like it's a positive for this recipe, it seems to be the case that the longer the patties cook, the drier they become.

- Hummus, Sriracha, and dill sauce are all great sauces to add to your falafel.

- Make this a Mediterranean hit with your family by add tabbouleh or olives to the menu.

# Nutritional Information:

This nutritional information is for one falafel patty.

| Calories | Fat | Sodium | Carbohydrates | Fiber | Sugar |
|---|---|---|---|---|---|
| 180 | 10 grams | 620 milligrams | 17.2 grams | 4.6 grams | 0.8 grams |

    This recipe can be interpreted as being the equivalent to an easy hamburger meal for the family. Just like when you cook a burger from scratch, this recipe requires you to form a patty and cook it on both sides before serving. Falafel is generally seen as a comfort food, but what differentiates this type of food from others that exist within this category is the healthy nature of falafel. Especially if you bake the falafel instead of fry it, you really can't go wrong with this recipe, especially if you opt to go without a bun or a pita and serve vegetable sides with this dish.

# Chapter 5: Recipes for Your Sweet Tooth

It's safe to say that one of the reasons why you're interested in the China Study Diet is because of its emphasis on a healthy lifestyle. While this is definitely a positive reason to start using this diet, it's also safe to assume that you're going to want a cheat day or two along the way, especially when you're first beginning to use the diet and it seems like you're going to be craving sugar for the rest of your life. While the China Study Diet certainly idealizes the average person's dieting goals, the fact of the matter is that we're all human at the end of the day. This chapter will present desserts that will indulge your sweet tooth while also adhering to the rules that the China Study Diet has put in place.

## Dessert Recipe 1: A Simple Fruit Blend

Level of Difficulty: 1

Preparation Time: 10 minutes

Serving Size: 4

## You Will Need:

- 1 cup fresh strawberries
- 1 cup fresh blueberries
- 1 cup fresh kiwi
- 1 cup seasonal fruit
- *Optional: Vegan whipped-cream*

## Appliances Needed:

- None

## Directions

The directions for this recipe are fairly straightforward. Cut up your fruit into bite-sized pieces and mix them into a medium-sized bowl. Once the fruit is adequately mixed so that there aren't too many of the same fruit in one spot in the bowl, refrigerate the bowl and serve once the fruit is chilled.

## Notes for this Recipe:

- While it's important to be strict with yourself while on any diet, especially when you're first beginning one, it's also important to realize that you will most likely need to gradually come into this diet, rather than dive in head-first. This being the case, you might want to consider treating yourself every so often. Of course, vegan whipped creams do exist and you can certainly dollop it in heaping amounts onto your fruit dessert, but the option also exists for you to forego a small aspect of the diet for one night and indulge in some good old fashioned Cool Whip.

## Nutritional Information:

This is the nutritional information for a fruit dessert without considering vegan whipped cream or Cool Whip.

| Calories | Fat | Sodium | Carbohydrates | Fiber | Sugar |
|---|---|---|---|---|---|
| 200 | 0 grams | 0 grams | 20 grams | 1 grams | 26 grams |

# Dessert Recipe 2: Frozen Fruit Cup

Level of Difficulty: 2

Preparation Time: 10 minutes, not counting the time it takes to freeze the fruit

Serving Size: 18 cups

## You Will Need:

- 1 can of orange juice concentrate, 6 ounces
- 1 can of frozen pineapple juice concentrate, 12 ounces
- 1 cup of sugar, preferably Stevia
- 3 firm bananas, sliced thinly
- 1 frozen package of strawberries, 16 ounces
- 1 can of mandarin oranges, 15 ounces, drained
- 1 can of crushed pineapple, 8 ounces

## Appliances Needed:

- 18 clear plastic cups

## Directions

For this recipe, you will be working with the concentrate first. Prepare the pineapple juice concentrate according to the instructions on the can first. Next, add the orange juice concentrate, sugar, lemon juice, fruit and water to the concentrate and spoon heaps of this mixture into the plastic cups after you've mixed up this combination. Place all of the cups together in a pan and place gingerly into the freezer. Ideally, these will stay in the freezer for between 40 to 50 minutes. When you're ready to serve, take out only the number that you need.

## Notes for this Recipe:

- This recipe is great for when you want to make a healthy dessert that can be easily made in advance. Think about it, if you make eighteen dessert cups for yourself or for your family, you could potentially have dessert for over a week.

## Nutritional Information:

This nutritional information represents the value of one individual fruit cup.

| Calories | Fat | Sodium | Carbohydrates | Fiber | Sugar |
|---|---|---|---|---|---|
| 179 | 0 grams | 8 milligrams | 100 grams | 6 grams | 44 grams |

# Dessert Recipe 3: Banana Bread Chocolate Chip Muffins

Level of Difficulty: 3

Preparation Time: 30 minutes

Serving Size: 16 muffins

## You Will Need:

- 2 cups whole wheat flour
- 1 and ½ teaspoon baking soda
- ½ teaspoon salt
- 1/3 cup canola oil
- 4 ripe bananas
- ¼ cup water
- 1 teaspoon vanilla extract
- *Optional:* 1 cup dark non-dairy chocolate chips

## Appliances Needed:

- A conventional oven

## Directions

Begin this recipe by preheating the oven to 350 degrees Fahrenheit. Next, make sure that you use non-stick cooking spray to coat your muffin tins to avoid the possibility of sticking. Next, mix the dry ingredients together, meaning the flour, the salt and the baking soda. In a separate bowl, mix together the sugar and the oil. Mash the ripe bananas and add the water and vanilla to the mashed bananas. If you're using chocolate chips in your recipe, also add them at this time. Mix the dry and the wet ingredients in with the mashed bananas. Everything should be evenly mixed, and the bananas should not be too lumpy. When you're satisfied with the mixing quality of the batter, begin pouring it into the muffin tins so that they are filled up three quarters of the way. Once the oven has preheated, place the tins in the oven and bake for about a half hour.

## Notes for this Recipe:

- For this particular recipe, you will want the ripest bananas possible. The riper the bananas, the sweeter the muffins will be in taste.

- You'll want to use Stevia or a no calorie sugar for this recipe in order to keep the caloric intake of this dessert to a minimum.

- It's advised that you use chocolate chips that don't contain dairy; however, the China Study Diet also promotes the idea of not being too crazily obsessed with the limitations of the diet. If you want some dairy in your chocolate chips, have it.

- This dessert can also be used as a breakfast food item in extreme moderation.

## Nutritional Information:

The nutritional information for this recipe is for one whole-wheat banana chocolate chip muffin.

| Calories | Fat | Sodium | Carbohydrates | Fiber | Sugar |
|---|---|---|---|---|---|
| 200 | 5 grams | 200 milligrams | 30 grams | 4 grams | 30 grams |

Of course, this breakfast item should not be made frequently because it is almost cake-like in consistency; however, it's certainly okay to indulge your sweet tooth every now and again. While the calorie count isn't too bad for this dessert item, it may appear that the sugar content is high. Due to the fact that you should have used Stevia for this recipe and not pure cane sugar, most of this sugar is from the sugar found in the banana, rather than the sugar found in sugar packets.

# Chapter 6: Soup Recipes to Warm Your Soul

While dessert can provide you with the opportunity to socialize with friends and put more fun into your diet, a hearty soup during the winter and fall months can provide you with plenty of comfort without a copious number of calories. Let's take a look at some of the soups that comply with the China Study Diet, so that you can trick your waistline into think it's indulging in more than it actually is.

## Soup Recipe 1: Nacho Soup with Vegetables

Level of Difficulty: 1

Preparation Time: 35 minutes

Serving Size: 4

## You Will Need:

- 2 cups of vegetable broth, preferably the low-sodium variety
- 1 cup of salsa, the chunkier the better
- 1 four-ounce can of diced green chilies, mild spiciness unless you like them hotter
- 2 fifteen-ounce cans of black beans, drained but not completely
- 2.5 cups of water

- 1 can of tomato paste

- 1/2 teaspoon of salt

- ½ teaspoon of pepper

- 1 teaspoon of cumin

- 3 diced garlic cloves

- ½ chopped onion, large

- 1 tablespoon of olive oil

- *Optional toppings:* Feel free to add tortilla chips to this recipe, as many as you'd like. Other toppings include cilantro, avocado, and vegan cheese or sour cream.

## Appliances Needed:

- A stovetop

## Directions

Find your largest pot and turn the stove on to medium-high heat. Once the pot has adequately heated up, add the olive oil to the pot and the garlic. Stir these two ingredients for about five minutes, or until the garlic looks transparent and slightly golden. Be sure to watch the garlic, and immediately remove it from its heat source if it starts to brown or burn. Once the garlic is well on its way, add the salt, the pepper, the cumin and the chili powder to the large pot. Then, add the water, the vegetable broth, the salsa, the green chilies, and the tomato paste. Stir these ingredients together so that they coat the garlic. Next, bring this combination to a simmer, throw in two cans of black beans with their liquid. Bring this mixture to a simmer once more. Once it reaches a simmer this time, reduce the heat of the stove to a low temperature and let stew for around twenty to thirty minutes. Once the ingredients are well-mixed and properly combined so that the flavor of the soup is savory, remove from heat. Serve with either your tortilla chips or other toppings that you've bought.

## Notes for this Recipe:

- Instead of using tomato paste for this recipe, you can instead use a 28-ounce can of diced tomatoes. If you opt to do this, you should use the liquid from the can of tomatoes and omit the 2.5 cups of water for which the original recipe calls.

- While you certainly can add vegan cheese or sour cream to this recipe because it's very likely that a key ingredient in a product like these will be soy, I would caution you to do so. If you start becoming too reliant on soy-based products, you'll start cutting corners on your diet. It's likely that you'll find yourself eating large amounts of prepared vegetarian and vegan foods, and this is not the point of the China Study Diet in any way shape or form. Stick to your principles, and consume vegan and vegetarian foods in low doses.

- As with any type of soup, you can certainly adjust the seasonings of your dish as-needed. Another great option is to add hot sauce if you enjoy heat.

## Nutritional Information:

This nutritional information is for one cup of soup, without any toppings.

| Calories | Fat | Sodium | Carbohydrates | Fiber | Sugar |
|---|---|---|---|---|---|
| 316 | 5.9 grams | 990 mg | 53 grams | 16 grams | 11 grams |

# Soup Recipe 2: Asparagus Soup with Crème

Level of Difficulty: 2

Preparation Time: 30 minutes

Serving Size: 4

## You Will Need:

- 1 ½ cups of vegetable broth
- 1-2 tablespoons of nutritional yeast
- 1 thinly-sliced shallot
- 4 minced cloves of garlic
- 10-ounces of fresh or frozen peas (this roughly comes out to about two cups of peas)
- 12-ounces of asparagus, trimmed so that the white ends are removed (this roughly comes to about one bundle of asparagus)
- Olive oil
- 1 ½ cups almond milk
- *Optional:* ½ juice of a lemon
- *For the croutons:* 2 cups of whole-wheat bread

- *For the croutons:* ¼ cup of olive oil

- *For the croutons:* ¼ teaspoon of garlic powder

- *For the croutons:* ¼ teaspoon of salt

- *For the croutons*: ¼ teaspoon of pepper

- *For the croutons:* ¼ teaspoon of dried oregano

- *For the croutons:* ¼ teaspoon of dried basil

## Appliances Needed:

- A conventional oven

## Directions

First, begin by preheating your oven to 400 degrees Fahrenheit. Spread your bundle of asparagus out on a baking sheet and drizzle your vegetables with olive oil. Additionally, also season these stalks lightly with salt and pepper. Toss the olive oil all over the asparagus until they are adequately coated. Next, once the oven has preheated, let the asparagus cook for about fifteen minutes. Once they're finished, set the asparagus aside for the time being. If you're making the croutons for this dish, the next step would be to reduce the heat of the oven from 400 degrees to 325 degrees. Moving our attention back towards the soup, while the oven is lowering in temperature, heat either a large saucepan or a medium-sized pot on the stovetop. Once whichever pan you've chosen to use is hot, add 2 tablespoons of olive oil, the shallot and the garlic. Season the shallot and the garlic with salt and pepper that adheres to your cooking preferences, and stir this mixture until everything in the pot or the saucepan is nicely coated. You should cook this combination for roughly two to three minutes, and your kitchen should be emanating a delicious and fragrant smell. Again, make sure that you're watching your garlic so that it doesn't burn or turn brown.

Once the shallots and the garlic have been prepped, add your peas, your vegetable broth, and your almond milk to the pot and season with even more salt and pepper. Let this cook for a few moments, and then transfer this entire mixture over to a blender. Don't forget to bring your asparagus with you! Blend all of these ingredients together, until the soup is extremely creamy and looks smooth to the eye. After you're satisfied with the quality of the blend for the soup, transfer it back to your pot on the stovetop. Add your nutritional yeast and whisk together with the other ingredients. Continue to cook this mixture at a simmer, and then reduce to low heat. Adjust as needed with seasoning.

Turning our attention back to the croutons, add the breadcrumbs to a mixing bowl and whisk together all of the seasonings with it. If you need to, throw a bit more garlic powder, salt and pepper into the bowl. Toss to coat the breadcrumbs. Spread the breadcrumbs onto a baking sheet and cook for between fifteen to twenty minutes. Remove from heat, and top the breadcrumbs over the soup for a dish that's truly enjoyable.

## Notes for this Recipe:

- You can opt to use avocado oil instead of olive oil for this recipe, although it's likely that avocado oil is going to be more difficult to find in the store compared to olive oil.

- The lemon juice in this recipe is used for merely aesthetic purposes. The lemon juice provides the soup with more brightness.

- The nutritional yeast is used to provide the asparagus soup with a cheesy flavor that cannot be obtained without it. While nutritional yeast is a great option when compared to vegan cheese, it can also be a bit difficult to work with. If you do use nutritional yeast in this recipe, know that you might need to trial this recipe a few times before you are happy with its turnout.

- If you're making this soup for company that you're having and you'd like to make this dish look a bit fancier, a great option is to reserve some of the asparagus that you're putting into the blender and save it as a garnish once the soup is finished.

## Nutritional Information:

This nutritional information is for ¼ of the recipe that was described above.

| Calories | Fat | Sodium | Carbohydrates | Fiber | Sugar |
|---|---|---|---|---|---|
| 143 | 5.5 grams | 652 milligrams | 16.4 grams | 6.5 grams | 5.9 grams |

# Conclusion

Thank You for making it through to the end of *The China Study Diet Cookbook: Plant-Based Whole Food Recipes for Every Taste!* Let's hope it was informative and was able to provide you with all the tools you need to achieve your goals whatever they may be. I truly hope that this book has demonstrated to you the fun that can exist in a diet that follows the rules of the China Study Diet. This diet doesn't have to be the most miserable experience that you've ever had. Rather, you can pick and choose ingredients from Chapter 1 that are of interest to you and use them in your everyday life.

The next step is to pick out a recipe from this book and experiment with it. Maybe at first, you follow the recipe exactly as you see it in this book, and then next time you tweak the recipe to best satisfy your individual palate. With this diet, the possibilities are endless with the ingredients that were discussed. Play around, and make this diet yours. Remember, a lifestyle change often lasts longer than does simply a diet regime.

Finally, if you found this book useful in anyway, a review on Amazon is always appreciated!

# Plant Based Diet:

*Transitioning to a Plant Based Diet for Better Health, Losing Weight, and Feeling Great*

© Copyright 2016 by Gabriel Montana - All rights reserved.

The following eBook is reproduced below with the goal of providing information that is as accurate and reliable as possible. Regardless, purchasing this eBook can be seen as consent to the fact that both the publisher and the author of this book are in no way experts on the topics discussed within and that any recommendations or suggestions that are made herein are for entertainment purposes only. Professionals should be consulted as needed prior to undertaking any of the action endorsed herein.

This declaration is deemed fair and valid by both the American Bar Association and the Committee of Publishers Association and is legally binding throughout the United States.

Furthermore, the transmission, duplication or reproduction of any of the following work including specific information will be considered an illegal act irrespective of if it is done electronically or in print. This extends to creating a secondary or tertiary copy of the work or a recorded copy and is only allowed with express written consent from the Publisher. All additional right reserved.

The information in the following pages is broadly considered to be a truthful and accurate account of facts, and as such any inattention, use or misuse of the information in question by the reader will render any resulting actions solely under their purview. There are no scenarios in which the publisher or the original author of this work can be in any fashion deemed liable for any hardship or damages that may befall them after undertaking information described herein.

Additionally, the information in the following pages is intended only for informational purposes and should thus be thought of as universal. As befitting its nature, it is presented without assurance regarding its prolonged validity or interim quality. Trademarks that are mentioned are done without written consent and can in no way be considered an endorsement from the trademark holder.

# Table of Contents

Introduction .................................................................... 1

Chapter 1: About the Plant Based Diet ........................................ 3

Chapter 2: How to Transition to Plant Based Eating .................. 8

Chapter 3: Your Eating Patterns .................................................. 14

Chapter 4: Evidence Based Nutrition ......................................... 20

Chapter 5: Breakfast Recipes ..................................................... 26

Chapter 6: Lunch Recipes .......................................................... 38

Chapter 7: Dinner Recipes ......................................................... 50

Chapter 8: Dessert Recipes ........................................................ 62

Conclusion ................................................................................. 72

# Introduction

Congratulations on downloading this book and thank you for doing so.

The following chapters will discuss how a plant based diet will be able to help you and some recipes that will allow you to get started with your plant based diet.

There are plenty of books on this subject on the market, thanks again for choosing this one! Every effort was made to ensure it is full of as much useful information as possible, please enjoy!

Learning about a plant based lifestyle can sometimes be difficult and time consuming. You may want to learn as much as you can about it as soon as you can, but it is important that you get accurate information so that you do not have to rely on sources that may not know what they are talking about. Learning as much as you can about the nutrition that goes into a plant based diet will help you to have a better time when you are making a transition.

It is not all about what you can or can't do when you are trying to eat a plant based diet. This book will teach you everything that you need to know about plant based and how it can benefit your body. It is something that you need to be able to enjoy when it comes to your diet, and you should use the book to make sure that you are doing the plant based diet the right way. The book will help you learn how to do it the right way.

The transition phase of switching to a plant based diet is often the hardest part. You must be careful that you are getting the most amount of nutrients possible and that you are doing it the right way. By following the transition advice in this book, you will be able to learn what you should do when you are thinking of switching…starting with the time when you first thought that you might be able to eat a plant based diet. The book has got your back.

All of the advice that is included in the book is backed up by science and has been taken right from the pages of the China Study and other studies that were done proving that a plant based diet is a great way to live for nearly anyone no matter what walk of life they are in. The book includes some valuable information about the studies that were done and what was found during these studies to help save you the hassle that would come with pursuing the studies on your own and trying to find the information.

When you are ready to make the switch or just want to try your hand at vegan cooking, the book will continue to be your guide. It includes recipes for breakfast, lunch, dinner and even desserts. You'll never run out of ideas for your meals when you read the book, and you have an idea of all of the different things that you can do with the plant based diet.

You will certainly be surprised with some of the delicious recipes that taste nothing like a plain salad and a lot of the information on the plant based diet that is found in the pages of this book.

# Chapter 1: About the Plant Based Diet

Before you make the leap to a fully plant based diet, you should first know a little about it. This chapter will serve as an introduction into the plant based diet, how it can benefit you and whether or not you can get healthy from eating a diet that revolves around only eating plants and plant products. By making sure that you know as much as possible before you get started, you'll be able to be more successful with it.

**What is a Plant Based Diet?**
The idea behind a plant based diet is that you eat food that only comes from plants. This doesn't mean that you only eat lettuce or fruits that are wrapped up in some form of a vegetable. It simply means that you eat foods that are *made* from plants. This means that you can eat soy, some grains, and even dairy-free alternative options.

When someone makes the decision to switch to a plant based diet, they may choose to reduce the amount of meat that they eat, but they may also completely eliminate the meat that they would normally consume from their diet. Most people who make the decision to start eating a plant based diet will also eschew foods that have been highly processed, including those that were originally plant based foods (like bleached flour).

Many plant based eaters do not start out full throttle. They work their way into a plant based diet, and they do this so that they will be able to make sure that they are doing it the right way. The first thing that most people do is begin to eat more plants and then slowly start to phase out the other foods that they would traditionally eat. The most common switch that is made while people are transitioning is to change from meat to legumes which often have close to the same amount of protein as meat would.

People who eat plant based diets do not have to only eat at home or survive on a diet of salads and fruit cups. They can eat out, they can eat nearly anything that they would like and the majority of people who try to stay strictly "plant based" will still eat meat or dairy every so often – although, once they have been plant based for a period of time, meat and dairy do not have the same appeal to them and can actually be hard on their stomachs.

As you learn more about plant based diets, you will find that there are many different reasons that someone would choose to eat only foods that come from plants. The reasons are numerous, but many people find that the accompanying benefits of it are enough to keep them eating a plant based diet for the rest of their lives.

**What are the Benefits of It?**
While different people may have different reasons for eating a plant based diet, there is no denying that plant based has a lot of great benefits for people. Whether you want to eat a plant based diet to help save the planet, because you don't like to see animals suffer or you simply want to do something that is healthy for yourself, you will be able to reap the benefits that come along with eating a diet that is centered around plants.

Consumer Reports has published information on the benefits of the plant based diet, and they reported that people who eat a plant based diet reduce their chances of dying early by around 19%. This is a huge number and can mean that you could literally add years onto your life just from eating a plant based diet. Their study included people who ate *mostly* plants but occasionally ate meat and dairy. Just imagine how much you could decrease your chances of dying early if you switched to an all plant diet instead of consuming meat or animal products occasionally.

Your chance of dying may be lowered because you will have healthier (and happier) heart levels. The reduced number of meat products that were included in the diet also led to a decrease in "bad" cholesterol which could be due to the reduction of animal fat in the diet. The American Journal of Cardiology showed that people who ate a diet that had mostly plants and very few sources of fat from meat or dairy were able to reduce their cholesterol by between 10 and 15 percent. They had almost complete success with lowering high numbers when they made the switch to a plant based diet.

Along with all of the other health benefits that come with a plant based diet, people who eat mostly plants have been happier when studies were conducted in their mental state while they are eating diets that are focused on plants instead of the traditional American diet that is heavy in saturated fats and meat products. Even people who had problems and mood disorders were able to be happier when they were eating plant based diets.

There are many more benefits, but a decreased chance of dying early, lower cholesterol and a more positive outlook on life are just a few of the benefits to eating a plant based diet. If those are not enough for you, you will be happy to learn that people who eat plant based are actually able to maintain a healthier weight than their counterparts who consume a large amount of meat in their diet on a regular basis.

**Can You Lose Weight?**
The question that weighs most heavily on people's minds is whether or not they are able to lose weight with a plant based diet.

It is important that people not confuse the word diet with the word...diet. A plant based diet is simply a way of eating and living while a diet in a different sense is a restricted way of eating to reduce the amount of weight or body fat. A plant based diet isn't a diet, it is a lifestyle that people with the intention of getting healthier all around.

There is no denying that the plant based diet is much healthier than some of the other methods of eating that people have when they are trying to improve their lives, but a plant based diet is not necessarily a diet plan that guarantees to help people lose weight in one way or another.

When people switch to a plant based diet, they do often see a drop in their weight. This is due to the fact that they are not eating a high amount of unhealthy fats and they are focusing more on eating calories that are nutritious instead of calories that are empty or do not provide them with the nutrients that they need. The weight loss that people see is generally secondary to the healthy changes that they will begin to see once they have started eating a plant based diet.

While it is important to understand that you will probably lose weight while eating a plant based diet, it is not a miracle cure that will do everything for you to be able to make you thinner or fit into those jeans that you wore in high school. It is a lifestyle, and you will need to change your entire way of thinking before you take it on. The weight loss benefits that come with eating a plant based diet should not be the first thing on your mind. You should be more focused on the fact that you are making your body healthier overall and you are reducing the risk of dying early.

Altogether, a plant based diet is one that has a lot of benefits and can even help you drop some weight. When you take on the lifestyle, you are able to eat anything that you want. Just because you eat a plant based diet does not mean that you can't occasionally have a piece of meat or some type of dairy product when you want it. It just means that you limit these products and make your diet all about the plants.

# Chapter 2: How to Transition to Plant Based Eating

Now that you know all of the health benefits that come with eating a plant based diet, you may be ready to dive right in so that you can start reaping those benefits. Take a break and slow down, though. You need to make sure that you do it the right way or you could end up *losing* nutrients that your body needs just because you want to get healthy. That would not be the right way to start your brand new journey.

**Get the Clearance**
Depending on your current lifestyle, it may not be the best decision for you to embark on a plant based journey right now. Your body may not be up to the demands, and you would never know that there was a problem and you started eating entirely plant based. You would feel the effects that come with some problems with your body quickly, and that could turn you off to living a plant based lifestyle. Making sure that you know what you are doing is imperative to be able to be successful. Making sure that your body is up to it is imperative to your own health.

For this reason, you need to make sure that your doctor knows that you are starting a plant based diet. Most doctors would be thrilled to hear that their patient is trying to take on a better lifestyle but you still need to let your doctor know ahead of time that you are planning to make a major change to your lifestyle. He or she will probably advise you to start slowly and to ease your way into it so that you do not shock your body with the major changes that come with eating mostly plants instead of mostly meats.

Do not be surprised if your doctor orders a battery of tests for you when you say that you are going to start a plant based diet. He or she will probably want to check your:
- Iron
- Blood glucose
- Cholesterol

These are just a few of the things that will help your doctor determine whether or not you are healthy enough to begin a plant based diet. Your doctor will also want to make sure that you are not pregnant because, while pregnant women *can* do well with plant based, it is not a good idea to start eating that way *while* you are pregnant.

**Add More Plants**
After you have the all clear from your doctor, you should consider the way that you are going to make the switch. Doing it slowly is the best way to go and will allow you to feel more comfortable with the changes that you are going to make in your life. You may become discouraged if you try to take on too much at one time.

The first thing that you should do is start adding more plants to your diet. For example, start eating a salad one day per week. The salad can even be the kind that has meat and dairy in it, just make sure that you are eating a salad with a lot of different vegetables in it. This will get you accustomed to the taste of vegetables and can help you to not feel like you are missing out when you make the full switch to a diet that doesn't have a lot of meat in it.

At this point, you do not want to trade any of your meals for plants. You just want to try adding some more plants to your diet. If you normally eat spaghetti, add some spinach to the noodles before you coat them in the sauce. If you normally eat your hamburgers plain, pile them high with tomatoes, pickles, and lettuce. These small additions will introduce healthy plants back into your body and will allow you to feel like you are just doing something small. The health benefits of a plant based diet will start to kick in as soon as you start to add more plants back into your diet.

While you are adding plants to your diet, always be on the lookout for new plants to try. If you've never tried a pomegranate before, pick one up at the grocery store and give it a try. If you've always wondered what a kale smoothie was really like, try it. Just make sure that you have a backup ready in case you don't like it. You may not want to replace your bacon and egg muffin with the kale smoothies just yet.

**Make One Switch**
After about one month of adding plants back into your diet, you should consider making the switch. Trade one meat product out of your diet each day into something that is plant based. This will help you to see what you will be eating in the future for the majority of your meals, but it will not be so big of a change that you feel overwhelmed with the idea of eating it all at the time.

One idea that is always good is to try to switch out a lunch sandwich with a salad. You can still use your dressing that you normally would. You can also even continue using your dairy toppings but just make sure that you are not getting meat on the salad. This meatless meal will still be just as filling as if it were meat but it will give you the chance to consume many more calories that are nutritious.

The salad that you trade out your lunchtime sandwich for doesn't have to just be boring limp lettuce thrown into a bowl with some ranch dressing. You can make any type of salad that you want. Start out with a bed of dark green romaine lettuce. Top it with tomatoes, cucumbers, shredded carrots, green peppers and red onions. The more colorful the salad, the more appealing it will be to you. Put some peanuts or walnuts on top to get some heart healthy fat that will keep you full for hours to come. If you love to try new things, you can even consider an apple strawberry salad. Mix your apples, strawberries, lettuce and other vegetables together for a unique flavor that has a burst of excitement in it while you are eating it.

It doesn't have to be all about salads, though. You can trade your dinner burger for a bean mix. You can switch out your normal morning bacon for a healthier fat – avocado. Cook your eggs *in* your avocado so that you can still enjoy the eggs, but you aren't missing out on anything when it comes to flavor. You will find that substituting one meal will help you to feel fuller and have a healthier lifestyle.

When you make the switch of one meal to a plant based meal, you will probably find that you will get many of the health benefits that come with a plant based diet – including weight loss.

**Try for One Day**
Studies have shown that taking one day out of the week and making it a day where you do not eat any meat can be almost as heart healthy as making a complete switch to a plant based diet. One day that is meatless and dairyless is a good idea because you will not only be able to have a better time with your plant based diet but you will also be able to save money because meat can be very expensive.

This phase should not be started until you are accustomed to doing one meal each day without meat. When you are doing a meatless day, you should continue substituting one meal out of each of the other days with plants instead of meat. This is a good idea to make sure that you are getting the most out of the transition.

Consider doing a Meatless Monday in your household. Make this for every family member while you are in the transition phase and keep it up even after you have moved on to being completely plant based. Your family will come to see it as a routine, and it will be the norm for them. Every family can benefit from a few more healthy options and do Meatless Monday is a popular switch. Consider all of the options that you have available to you when you are doing the switch.

When you are doing this part of the process, make sure that you do not eat meat or dairy for the full day. This can be difficult at first, so you may want to start out with just meat and later on eliminate the dairy from your diet during that day. It is a good idea to do this so that you do not get overwhelmed and so that you don't have to worry about doing too much at one time. Consider all of the options that you have available to you before you start out so that you are prepared with the right substitutes for the meat.

Do this for a month. Once you have done one day that is complete without meat for one month, you can consider adding another day in. Do this slowly until you go the entire week without eating meat. Remember, though that it is alright to take a break from it. Eating a small amount of meat or dairy is not going to throw off the health benefits that you get from eating a diet that is focused mostly on plants.

## Amp Up Your Substitutions

Once you have transitioned completely to a plant based diet, you will want to consider some of the other options that are available to you. There are many things that you can do to trade out for meat, and you don't have to live on a diet of lettuce and carrots – you're not a rabbit.

Make sure that you are getting enough protein in your diet. You can do this by eating things like beans and grains that have protein in them. You should also make sure that you are getting enough fat in your diet. Things like olive oil and avocados will be able to give you the fat that you need without causing major damage in the way that fat from meat does. This is something that is important because fat can be used as a fuel to help your body function throughout the day.

It is always a good idea to try something new. You started the plant based lifestyle because you wanted to get healthier. Part of health is having a large variety of different things that you can eat when you are trying to maintain the healthy lifestyle. Don't be afraid to try new things because they may end up becoming your favorite food. Try new plants, try the commercial vegan food and even consider trying things that you never would have done.

One thing to keep in mind is that soda is *not* plant based. Your best options for drinking when you are on the plant based diet is to stick to water, coffee that is plain and tea that is all natural. The drink selections may be boring to you so you may want to consider this part as the final phase of your switch to plant based. You can also consume alcohol since most of it *is* plant based, but be wary of drinks that have extremely high sugar counts or are mixed with other things.

# Chapter 3: Your Eating Patterns

When you begin to eat a plant based diet, you may realize that your eating habits will begin to change. You may eat less or more than you used to and you may find that you need to eat les to be able to fill you up in the way that you used to have to eat a lot to be filled up. Your body will change, too. You may find that, if you do eat meat, you are unable to tolerate it in the way that you once were able to. This can be a clear indicator that the plant based diet is working to help you have a healthier life.

It is important that you get the same nutrition that you got when you were eating a meat and dairy filled diet. Just because you no longer eat meat or dairy does not mean that you have to suffer and get less nutrition than you used to. You may find that you are having some difficulty getting the nutrition that you need when you are on a plant based diet, but there are plenty of options for people who struggle to get exactly what they need from it.

**Protein**
For most Americans, the majority of their protein comes from the meats that they eat. Since they eat diets that are heavy in meat, they may not be able to figure out how to get enough protein when they start to eat a diet that is based on plants. It is important, however, that they continue to get a healthy amount of protein so that they will be able to make sure that they are getting the right nutrients for their bodies.

Protein comes in many forms, but you will most likely find it in nuts and legumes. They are packed with protein, and some of the legumes that you can consume will even have more protein per gram than some of the meat that you would have eaten before you switched to a plant based diet. It is important to know which beans and nuts are best for you.

Things like hummus, black beans, and peanut butter should play a big role in the diet that you consume while you are eating only plants. These are highest in protein and will be able to help you have a better time with the way that you get protein sources.

If you find that you are lacking in protein, it may be necessary to incorporate a small amount of meat or eggs back into your diet. You may consider eating an egg for breakfast one or two days a week to help you get the protein that you need. While eggs are, technically, meat, it may be easier for you to consume eggs than it would be for your plant adjusted body to try to digest a large steak.

**Fats**
Since the majority of Americans do consume dairy and it makes up a big part of their diet, they are able to get the fat that they need from that. What fat they don't get from the dairy products that they regularly consume, they are able to get from the meat that they eat. These are both big factors when it comes to switching to plant based. If people are not worried about the protein aspect of their diet, the chances are that they are worried whether or not they are getting enough fat in their diet.

While it may be easy and almost second nature for you to think of fats as bad, they are actually good for you. The right kind of fat can help you to get the nutrition that you need, and it can help you make sure that you stay fuller for a longer period of time. The body burns fat that you consume easily and it can convert it into energy. It is for this reason that athletes who are preparing for a big game or another event will eat a small amount of fat right before they begin so that they are able to stay satiated throughout the entire time that they are performing as athletes.

People who eat only plants are able to get their fats from healthy sources. Avocados are one of the most popular options for people who want to have healthy fats in their diet. They are easy to eat, do not require much cooking and can be flavored in several different ways. They even have a taste that is flavorful on its own for people to be able to consume. They are versatile and can be eaten with nearly every meal that you consume. Another way that plant based dieters are able to get the fat that they need is to cook their vegetables in oil. Just because you are eating a plant based does not mean that you have to eat it all raw. You can cook your vegetables in healthy fats like olive oil and coconut oil.

**Eating Meals**
When you switch to a plant based diet, you may find that your meal schedule is slightly different than what it once was when you were eating meats and dairy products. This change should be expected, and you need to prepare to adjust your schedule accordingly so that you get the right amount of nutrition when it comes to the way that you eat.

When you are eating a plant based diet, you may be more likely to eat more at one sitting. This nutrition will act as fuel and will keep you powered until the next day. Since you are eating nutrient dense food, you may find that you have to eat less often than what you did when you were eating a diet that was focused primarily around meat and dairy. This is something that can make things easier on you because you won't have to eat nearly as much

On the contrary, you may find that you are hungrier than what you were when you were eating a meat based diet. This is more common at the beginning of your transition to a plant based lifestyle, but it can happen at any point. If you find that you are a lot hungrier than you were before, you may want to consider upping your fat or protein intake. These can help you stay fuller for longer and will make you feel more satisfied. You may also want to space your meals closer together so that you don't have to worry about getting very hungry and eating too much at the next meal.

**Cooking Out Nutrition**
When you are eating a plant based diet, you automatically get more fresh nutrients than you would if you were eating a meat based diet, but you must make sure that you are eating the vegetables in the right way. Raw vegetables will be best for you, but if you want to cook your vegetables, there are certain ways that can be better than others so that you will be able to make sure that you are getting the largest number of nutrients out of the vegetables and fruits.

One way that you can be sure that you are always getting the most out of your vegetables is to steam them instead of cooking them any other way. This will simply heat them up and make them more tender. It will not cook any of the nutrients out of them, and they will still remain pretty crunchy so that they have the distinctive vegetable texture. Make sure that you have a steamer that works well with the vegetables so that you don't overcook them in the steamer.

Cooking your vegetables in any way is still better than not eating plants, but sautéing is the worst way to cook your vegetables. If you are looking for a way to get your healthy fats in, this can work to your advantage but aside from that you are simply cooking out the nutrients and coating the vegetables in fat that will be harder to digest. You do need to get your fat from somewhere but just make sure that you are not completely destroying the vegetables. Some sautéing is alright but don't cook every single vegetable that you eat in that way.

## Supplements

As hard as you may try to make sure that you are doing well with your plant based diet, it may still be difficult for you to get all of the nutrients that you need. For this reason, you may want to consider supplements, but you should always talk to your doctor before you begin taking any type of supplement to make sure that you are doing what you are supposed to do and to ensure that you are not going to make yourself sick from the supplements. Some supplements that people who eat plant based diets regularly take are:

- Iron
- B12
- Vitamin K
- Magnesium
- Vitamin C
- Calcium

All of these are in different plants, but you may have trouble making sure that you are getting all of them into your diet. It can be difficult to get them, and you may have to eat a lot more than what you normally would be able to get them in your diet, but supplements can make it much easier to get them since they are easy to take and they get absorbed into the body.

Talking with your doctor before starting supplements is always a good idea. Some supplements may only be available by prescription and others may have interactions with the medications that you take. Talking to your doctor before beginning a supplement regime will ensure that you are not taking something that could be harmful to your body.

**Regular Checkups**

People who eat plant based diets are more susceptible to health problems like low iron which can lead to anemia. This is a relatively easy condition to treat, but you need to make sure that your doctor is aware of it before it gets out of hand. There are many different things that you can do to make sure that you are getting proper nutrition but always checking with your doctor will be able to help you the most.

Scheduling regular checkups are important in any case but can be even more beneficial for people who are eating a plant based diet. Make sure that you schedule the checkup and actually go to it so that you will be able to reap the benefits that come with visiting the doctor. Your doctor may order blood tests or even do a physical exam to make sure that you are getting all of the nutrients that you need.

The purpose of a plant based diet is to make your life healthier. Be sure that your doctor knows why you are doing that and that your doctor can help you with it. Without professional medical help behind you, you may become sick or may go in the opposite direction of healthy even though that was the point of starting a plant based diet.

# Chapter 4: Evidence Based Nutrition

There is a lot of evidence that a plant based diet may be the best option for you. This evidence comes not only in the form of proof of people who have done it but also in scientific studies that have been conducted on it. While no one diet is going to be the healthiest option for every person in the world, the plant based diet has had excellent results for people who want to be able to get healthy and cut some of the processed foods out of their diet.

Among the studies, scientists found that there were many different benefits and very few problems that were associated with plant based diets. The biggest benefits came in the form of heart health while the biggest problems were in the form of problems with low iron and low absorption of other vitamins that could be easily fixed with supplements.

**The China Study**
The China study was a study that was conducted to prove (or disprove) that the plant based diet would be able to help reduce heart disease and other health problems in people. The study was then published into a book that was easy for the layman to be able to read.

While the study aimed to show that people were less likely to have heart disease as a result of eating a diet comprised mostly of plants, in the end, it offered so much more and proved that there were many more health benefits for people who made a choice to eat only a plant based diet.

The study was performed over a series of many years, and it involved data from decades ago. It took into account the fact that the United States is a very unhealthy place and that many more people who come from the United States are much more susceptible to things like heart disease and diabetes. In other countries, these things are nearly nonexistent, and they certainly do not happen as early as what they do in the United States. What the study also uncovered? The United States was one of the biggest consumers of meat and dairy products in the world. The study was able to link a connection between the two with the way that things lined up and with the data that came directly from participants in the study.

One of the first things that the study was able to prove is that a plant based diet was able to significantly reduce the likeliness of diabetes in patients who ate only vegan foods. This was something that was relatively surprising to most because it had long been thought that plants, like grains and even wheat, were the cause of diabetes. It turns out that the administrators of the study were able to prove that eating a diet that is high in meat and dairy fat can actually be the contributing factor for diabetes.

Places like China had a very low rate of heart disease and diabetes. They also had a much higher life expectancy when it came to food-related diseases in this area. What was interesting is that people in China consume mainly plant based diets. They do eat some seafood, but their meat consumption overall is much less than the United States. Their red meat consumption was much lower than other countries from around the world, and they were one of the leaders when it came to lowering diabetes and heart disease statistics.

People who thought they were safe eating a strict vegetarian diet turned out to be wrong, too. What was commonly thought of as "safe" for vegetarians, by products of animals – like milk, was proven to be detrimental to the body when this study was performed. Milk was one of the number one things studied in the book. The study helped to uncover that not only did milk act as insulin and promote diabetes within the body but it also made people much more susceptible to cancer. The study found that humans were *so* sensitive to casein that is found in milk that simply cutting off the supply of dairy products to people was enough to kill cancer cells. The study also did it in reverse and introduced milk back into the diet which rapidly increased the growth of cancer in the body. It proved that other sources of calcium were just as effective at making bones strong and kids grow as milk was, with the added benefit that people did not get cancer from naturally grown vegetables.

For years, health food afficianados have been fighting the war on pesticides on food, but it turns out that they are fighting the wrong battle. The China study was able to open the eyes of some more people with this portion of the study. What is even more worrying is that meat and dairy products nearly triple the amount of cancer growth than pesticides on naturally occurring food does. The China study essentially said that people who are concerned about their health should be more focused on cutting meat and dairy out of their diet instead of cutting things out that could have the possibility of a slight residue from pesticides (in which case, they could just wash it thoroughly before consuming). Eating organically does not hurt things, but there is no point in eating organically or all naturally if people are going to still consume detrimental health products like meat and dairy products.

Since the 1970's, people religiously followed Dr. Atkins and the war that he had set up on carbohydrates. The China study also proved that Dr. Atkins was *not* correct in his method of thinking. While cutting out carbs can help people to lose weight, the large amount of meat and dairy that is consumed during this diet can have even more detrimental side effects than being morbidly obese can. Instead, the China Study found that people who ate a *reasonable* amount of carbs in addition to the food that they were consuming that was mostly plant based were the way to go. The carbs that are consumed should be from naturally occurring plants and should not have any meat or dairy (including eggs) products that are in them to stay in line with the findings from the study and to get the biggest health benefit from them.

The biggest problem that the China Study found with a plant based diet was that people had low iron with it. This was something that came from not eating the right vegetables to get the amount of iron that they needed to be able to survive. While iron is an essential nutrient that everyone needs to be able to live, it is something that is often overlooked even by people who eat meat. The China Study revealed that simply increasing some vegetables that were high in iron or placing participants on iron supplements was enough to drastically raise their red blood cell counts, a clear indicator of the iron in their blood. It also found that cooking with a cast iron skillet, even when using plant based oils, people would be able to increase their iron intake.

Possibly one of the most surprising aspects of the study is in finding what humans really are. For a very long time, people thought that humans needed both meat and vegetables to be able to survive. They were classified as omnivores, but it was actually discovered during the study that people are simply herbivores who have added animal fats into their diet for purposes other than nutrition. While they are able to eat the animal byproducts with no immediate problems, they do pose problems for herbivores in the years to come. There are *no* nutrients in meat that you can't get from plants that are already found on this earth.

One thing that the study does not go over is that there are animals on the planet who are true omnivores or even carnivores. For example, dogs are carnivores. Some people who live a vegan lifestyle try to replace their dog's nutrition with plant based nutrition – this is a terrible idea because dogs do, in fact, need the nutrients that come from meat and have a hard time digesting non animal sources of both proteins and fats for their bodies to be able to use for fuel. Essentially, meat for humans is bad. Meat for Dogs is good.

The China Study came up with many great ideas about nutrition, what it means for the human race and what it can do for your body. It is important that people take the information in the China Study with the value that it holds. You should always form your own opinion on nutrition and be sure that you check with your doctor before you take on any type of major lifestyle change, but you should also consider the inarguable results that were found in the China Study.

**Following the Plant Based Diet**
Aside from the China Study, there have been many other studies that were performed and that had great results proving that the plant based diets may be one of the best diets available for people to follow if they are trying to live their life in the most natural way possible. Universities like Cornell and Oxford have all done studies on it, and the conclusions have always been that the diets were among the best ways for people to eat with very few problems seen within the diets.

The studies combined with the knowledge that you have received from this book may be enough to help convince you that a plant based diet is the way to go. When you are ready to get started with your plant based diet, make sure that you talk to your doctor.

Once you have the all-clear on the medical end, you need to get started slowly. You cannot just jump into a vegan lifestyle without looking back.

Begin immersing yourself in vegetables and other plant based foods. This will take some time but do not get discouraged. Slipping up and eating meat once in a while will not harm you in the long term, but it is a good idea to make sure that your diet is filled with vegetables, fruits, and other plants. You will be healthier, happier and will have a better chance at living for a longer time.

It may be hard for you to get started with a plant based diet or even getting an idea of what you can eat while you are living a plant based lifestyle. For that reason, we have included some wonderful and delicious vegan recipes for you to follow. These recipes are both easy and will give you the chance to see what it is like to live a plant based lifestyle. There are many options that are available to you so that you can choose from your favorite breakfasts, lunches, dinners and even desserts – without a single animal product consumed throughout your day.

# Chapter 5: Breakfast Recipes

Breakfast is often regarded as the most important meal of the day, and things are no different if you are following a plant based diet. Make sure that you eat a filling breakfast so that you will not get hungry throughout the day. A breakfast that is high in proteins and even some fat will help to keep you satisfied until it is time for you to eat lunch.

# Breakfast Recipe 1: Oatmeal – Elvis Style

Level of Difficulty: 1

Preparation Time: 20 minutes

Serving Size: 2 bowls of oatmeal

## You Will Need:

- 1 tbsp of peanut butter, all natural if possible
- ½ cup of water
- 1 cup of oats that are steel cut
- ¼ of a tsp of vanilla extract
- 1 large banana that is ripe

## Appliances Needed:

- A stove
- A pot

## Directions

Start cooking by boiling your water until it reaches a rolling boil. Alternatively, you can make the oatmeal by nuking it in the microwave but it may get soggier quicker, and it may cause the oatmeal to become unappetizing to eat. Once the water is boiling, put your steel cut oats in the water. It should take about

5-10 minutes to fully cook depending on the oats and the temperature of your water. Once the oatmeal is done the cooking, transfer it to two bowls that have been prepared. Stir in the vanilla and the peanut butter until they are thoroughly mixed up. Slice the banana and divide it among the two different bowls. Serve hot.

## Notes for this Recipe:

- If you find that the oatmeal is not sweet enough for you, you can use agave nectar or another plant based sweetener. Avoid using honey because it is an animal product. You can use sugar, but the sugar may cause you to burn off the energy that is provided by the peanut butter and the banana much more quickly.

## Nutritional Information:

This is the nutritional information for one serving of the recipe.

| Calories | Fat | Sodium | Carbohydrates | Fiber | Sugar |
|---|---|---|---|---|---|
| 323 | 15 | 10 | 65 | 14 | 3 |

The nutritional information shows that there is a nice ratio of carbohydrates and fat in the recipe. It is a great option for every day or for a treat in the morning. The oatmeal recipe will, obviously, have different nutritional information if you decide to add sugar to it or any other type of sweetener. Make sure that you adjust that according to what you have decided to add to it.

# Breakfast Recipe 2: Classic Avocado Toast

Level of Difficulty: 1

Preparation Time: 20 minutes

Serving Size: 2 pieces of toast

## You Will Need:

- 1 avocado
- 2 slices of vegan bread
- ¼ of a tsp of lime juice
- ¼ of a tsp of salt
- ¼ of a tsp of pepper

## Appliances Needed:

- A toaster

## Directions

To start the recipe, you should cut your avocado. The proper way to cut your avocado is to slice it from end to end using an extra sharp knife. Cut on both sides and connect the cuts. Twist the top and the bottom of the avocado so that it comes apart cleanly. Lay the side that has the pit into it on your counter and put the blade of your knife into the pit. Lift it out. It should lift out easily. Remove from your knife and throw the pit away. Cut the avocado in a diced pattern on each side of it. Use a spoon to get underneath the flesh of it and slide it out of the skin. Put it into a bowl. Meanwhile, put your bread in the toaster and toast it until it is done the way that you like it. Mash your avocado into the bowl and add the lime juice, the salt, and the pepper. If you desire, you can also add some tomato, onion and a pinch of garlic powder to it to give it some extra flavor.

## Notes for this Recipe:

- Avocado toast is such a versatile meal, especially for breakfast. You can combine this with your favorite fruit in the morning and have energy that lasts all day. You can top avocado toast with virtually anything that you want, and you can make it so that it will suit any taste. The avocado has a mild flavor to it and can complement nearly any flavors.

## Nutritional Information:

This is the nutritional information for one serving of the recipe.

| Calories | Fat | Sodium | Carbohydrates | Fiber | Sugar |
|---|---|---|---|---|---|
| 458 | 39 | 135 | 26 | 13 | 1.8 |

While it may appear that this recipe has a lot of fat in it, don't be scared of the fat. Not only is it the healthy fat that you need to get all of the nutrition to be able to survive, but it is also able to hold you over until lunch. Avocados have just the right fat that you need in your plant based diet to be able to help you get all of the nutrients and energy.

# Breakfast Recipe 3: The Night Before Breakfast Bake

Level of Difficulty: 1

Preparation Time: overnight

Serving Size: 6 servings

## You Will Need:

- 3 apples
- 2 cups of oats that are steel cut
- ¼ of a tsp of salt
- ½ of a cup of sugar
- ½ of a tsp of cinnamon
- ¼ of a tsp of apple pie spice
- ¼ of a cup of apple juice

## Appliances Needed:

- A slow cooker

## Directions

Begin by slicing up the apple. You can cut it so that it is in chunks or you can cut it so that it is in slices. The size can be however large you want it to be so that you will be able to enjoy it in the recipe. Do not worry about taking the skin off of the apples but do make sure that you take the stem and the seeds out of the apple. You can use an apple corer to be able to do this. You can also do it manually. Mix the rest of the ingredients in a bowl together and make sure that they are combined so that there are no major clumps. If you want it to be a little more doughy, you can add 1 or 2 tablespoons of whole wheat flour or any flour of your choice to the bake. This will help it to have a better taste and can make it seem more like it just came fresh out of the oven. Spray down your slow cooker with a light spray of vegan cooking oil or just rub it down with coconut oil. Place all of your ingredients that have already been mixed up into the slow cooker and put it on low setting. Let it cook for 8-10 hours, overnight. The longer that you let it cook, the more tender the apples become.

## Notes for this Recipe:

- This breakfast bake is always a good idea because it requires minimal effort on your part. All you need to do is go to bed to be able to wake up to a nutritious and filling breakfast. Make sure that you prepare your ingredients the night before and begin cooking it so that you don't have to do anything in the morning. This is great for people who are on the go in the morning or need something that they can just grab on their way out of the door. The recipe can include any fruits that you like, and you can make substitutions to make it taste better for you and your family.

## Nutritional Information:

This is the nutritional information for one serving of the recipe.

| Calories | Fat | Sodium | Carbohydrates | Fiber | Sugar |
|---|---|---|---|---|---|
| 382 | 3.1 | 113 | 43.6 | 12.1 | 40 |

This breakfast recipe is packed with sugar which makes it the perfect recipe if you are craving something sweet. The sweetness of the apples combined with the sugar and the other ingredients can make it even more delicious for you to be able to eat. This is something that will be great for you if you want something that is sweet. It can even work as a dessert instead of breakfast. If you are using it as a breakfast, the carbohydrates and the sugar in it will help give you a lot of energy throughout your day.

# Breakfast Recipe 4: Not Eggs and Potatoes

Level of Difficulty: 3

Preparation Time: 15 minutes

Serving Size: 2 bowls of eggs

## You Will Need:

- ¼ of a block of tofu
- Chili powder
- ¼ of a tsp of salt
- ¼ of a tsp of pepper
- 1 potato
- 1/2 of a tsp of vegetable oil

## Appliances Needed:

- Stove
- Skillet

## Directions

You should begin cooking this recipe by preparing your tofu. Put the block into a mixing bowl and use a hand mixer until the tofu resembles the way that scrambled eggs would look when they are cooked. It should be slightly crumbly but not to the point where it begins to mix back together with itself. You should then peel and cut the potato until it is in very small diced pieces. You can even use frozen diced potatoes if you want to cheat on the recipe or to save yourself some time. Put your stove onto medium high heat and pour your vegetable oil or other oil into the pan. You can then put your tofu and your potatoes into the pan and sprinkle them with the seasonings. Stir to mix up all of the seasonings with the potatoes and the tofu. This will allow the flavors to combine and can help make it more aromatic. Cook until the potatoes are tender and divide into two bowls. Serve while it is still hot.

## Notes for this Recipe:

- You don't have to use just chili powder in this recipe. You can use southwest seasoning, garlic powder or any other type of seasoning that you like. Just be sure that the seasoning that you use does not have any hidden animal byproducts in it so that you do not end up blowing your plant based diet. If you want to make the recipe with less fat in it, forgo the vegetable oil and use a nonstick skillet instead so that you do not have to worry about it getting stuck to the pan *or* using oil in it that can make the fat count even higher. You can add onions, peppers or even tomatoes to it if you would like to have a full array of different macronutrients included in your breakfast.

## Nutritional Information:

This is the nutritional information for one serving of the recipe.

| Calories | Fat | Sodium | Carbohydrates | Fiber | Sugar |
|---|---|---|---|---|---|
| 228 | 5.9 | 19 | 15.4 | 2.2 | 2 |

The recipe should stay about the same in the nutrition department when it comes to the changes that you make. Minor changes to the recipe, like the spices that you use, will not change the nutritional information. If you add anything to the recipe, like vegetables, you should be sure to count all of the extra calories that it will have in it.

# Chapter 6: Lunch Recipes

Lunch can be tricky, especially when you are trying to eat a plant based diet. It may be more beneficial for you to make sure that you have lunches prepared ahead of time so that you don't leave yourself without a nutritious lunch that you can enjoy whether you are at work or on the go. These lunch recipes will help you to stay full throughout the work day so that you don't need to worry about loading up on bad for you food at dinner.

# Lunch Recipe 1: Vegetable Soup with Extra Spices

Level of Difficulty: 2

Preparation Time: 3 hours

Serving Size: 6

## You Will Need:

- Water, 3 cups
- 12 oz of mixed vegetables of your choice
- 4 large potatoes
- 12 oz of frozen California vegetables
- ¼ of a tsp of gr black pepper
- ½ of a tbsp of oregano
- ½ of a cup of quinoa that is rinsed
- 1 tin can of red beans
- 1 tin can of Italian style diced tomatoes
- 1 tin can of white beans or navy beans

## Appliances Needed:

- A stove
- A stock pot

## Directions

Peel your potatoes and cut them up into sixths so that they will be large enough to add substance to the soup but not too large that you cannot enjoy the soup as result of them. Make sure that you do not thaw out the frozen vegetables because they will become overcooked and this can be a problem. You want them to be tender, but you don't want them to be too tender that they lose their flavor and their texture. Make sure that you do not drain the liquid out of each of the cans of beans because that will add to the overall liquid in the recipe. All you need to do is put your pot on the stove and put it on low to medium heat. Add all of the ingredients that you have prepared to the soup and mix well. Cook on the stove for at least three hours but longer if you want your potatoes and other vegetables to get as tender as possible. You can divide this and eat it right after cooking, or you can make the decision to do it before you go to work.

## Notes for this Recipe:

- If you make the recipe to take with you to work or for later on, make sure that you use a thermos or some other way to keep it hot. You can also microwave it while you are at work but just make sure that it is heated the whole way through. The soup will taste the best when it is hot or, at least, heated up to room temperature. There are many more vegetables that you could put in the soup so put any in that you would like to make it taste the way that you want.

## Nutritional Information:

This is the nutritional information for one serving of the recipe.

| Calories | Fat | Sodium | Carbohydrates | Fiber | Sugar |
|---|---|---|---|---|---|
| 266 | 7 | 212 | 13 | 4.3 | 3.8 |

This recipe is low calorie, but studies have shown that soups are better able to fill people up and that they may be your best option when you are trying to make the food that you eat last. It is important to note that the more vegetables that you put in the soup, the more calories it will be but also the more filling it will so load it up with all of the vegetables that you can to make the best and most filling vegetable soup.

# Lunch Recipe 2: Chick Pea Pita Pocket

Level of Difficulty: 2

Preparation Time: 20 minutes

Serving Size: 1

## You Will Need:

- 2 pita pockets that have already been cooked
- ½ of can of chickpeas that have been rinsed and drained
- 2-3 pieces of romaine lettuce
- ½ of a cucumber that is sliced
- ½ of a tomato that is diced
- 1 of a tsp of buffalo sauce

## Appliances Needed:

## Directions

Once your chickpeas have been rinsed and drained, coat them in the buffalo sauce so that they will be able to have the flavor. If you do not like buffalo sauce, you can use any type of hot sauce, spices or any other vegan sauce that you like to give them a flavor. It will help you to have a more enjoyable lunch if there is a flavor to it beyond what the vegetables provide. Begin stuffing your pita pockets with the lettuce and then top with the tomatoes, the cucumber and the chickpeas that have been coated in the sauce. Serve cold or room temperature if you are unable to keep it in the fridge.

## Notes for this Recipe:

- When you are making this, you can add any vegetables that you like. You don't have to use the cucumber and tomato, and you can add green peppers, onion and even carrots to the pita pocket to give it a flavor that is distinct. While the sauce helps to keep it from tasting so dry while you are eating it, you can substitute the sauce with any spices that you would like. The pita pockets are completely customizable, and you can make sure that they will be able to suit your own taste.

## Nutritional Information:

This is the nutritional information for one serving of the recipe.

| | Calories | Fat | Sodium | Carbohydrates | Fiber | Sugar |
|---|---|---|---|---|---|---|
| | 534 | 5.1 | 276 | 102 | 19.8 | 3.3 |

Different pita pockets will have different fat and carbohydrate count. While it may be tempting to choose the one with the lowest nutritional information to it, you may want to consider a higher carbohydrate and fat count so that you can maintain energy throughout the day. This will help you to stay full and satisfied without worrying about taking a break to eat a snack.

# Lunch Recipe 3: Quesadilla

Level of Difficulty: 3

Preparation Time: 20 minutes

Serving Size: 1

## You Will Need:

- 2 tortilla that do not have meat byproducts
- 1 avocado
- 1 small tomato
- 1 full teasp of coconut oil

## Appliances Needed:
- Stove
- Pan

## Directions

Start by cutting your avocado. Remove the pit and dice it so that it is easier to scoop out. Mash it up by using a fork. Meanwhile, heat up your coconut oil in the pan and make sure that it is not boiling over. You only want it to be on low to medium heat. Cut your tomato up into small pieces that will be able to fit easily into your quesadilla. Spread your tortilla with the avocado and sprinkle it with tomato. Carefully put your tortilla that is covered with the ingredients into the pan and heat it up. Lay your second tortilla on top of the first. You only need to cook it for a couple of minutes on each side until your tortillas become golden brown.

## Notes for this Recipe:

- If you have it on hand or you want your quesadilla to have a different flavor, you can add some soy cheese to the quesadilla so that you are able to make it stick together better. It will not melt in the way that dairy cheese would but it will give your quesadilla a little more substance. You can also add onions and peppers to the mixture of avocados and tomatoes so that you are able to do more with it. An addition of taco seasoning or garlic powder to the avocado can also increase the flavor with a minimal amount of effort involved. Note that not all tortillas that you find will be vegan or will be able to suit the needs of your plant based diet. Make sure that you find one that does not contain any egg products or anything that is a byproduct of an animal.

## Nutritional Information:

This is the nutritional information for one serving of the recipe.

| Calories | Fat | Sodium | Carbohydrates | Fiber | Sugar |
|---|---|---|---|---|---|
| 505 | 45.2 | 37 | 41.1 | 17.2 | 3.1 |

This may seem like a lot of calories that you would be consuming for lunch, but it is important to note that it is something that you will need to be able to nourish you until you eat dinner. The combination of good fat from the avocado with the carbohydrates from the tortillas will give you the energy that you need to stay fueled. You will be surprised to find that you probably will not even need to eat a snack in between lunch and dinner.

# Lunch Recipe 4: Lentil Tiki Masala

Level of Difficulty: 3

Preparation Time: 6 hours

Serving Size: 6

## You Will Need:

- 2 cups of red lentils
- 1 large tin can of diced tomatoes that are *not* Italian style
- 1 tbsp of garam masala
- 1 tsp of ginger
- 1 tsp of turmeric
- 1 tsp of garlic
- 1 small onion that is yellow

## Appliances Needed:
- Slow cooker

## Directions

You can use any type of lentil that you want, but the red adds a nice touch of color to the dish. Make sure that you use dried lentils so that they do not get overcooked when you are using your slow cooker. The dried lentils will be able to stand up better in the way that you are cooking everything. Cut the onions up into small diced pieces and add all of the ingredients into your slow cooker. Make sure that it is stirred up so that all of the flavors get mixed together and so that you are able to make sure that the spices are incorporated in the best way possible. Once it is all in the slow cooker, cover it and cook on low for 4-6 hours or until the lentils are tender enough for you to be able to eat.

## Notes for this Recipe:

- It is important to nut use Italian style diced tomatoes because the Italian spices will not work well with the spices that are in the garam masala. They will contradict each other and can create a strange flavor. Once this is done, you can top it with cilantro. If you have any plant based faux yogurt on hand, you can mix the yogurt with cucumbers and tomatoes with a sprinkle of cilantro for a great topping to this dish.

## Nutritional Information:

This is the nutritional information for one serving of the recipe.

| Calories | Fat | Sodium | Carbohydrates | Fiber | Sugar |
|---|---|---|---|---|---|
| 257 | 1.0 | 11 | 45.3 | 21.5 | 5.6 |

There are many different variations to this recipe. You can replace the lentils with nearly anything from tofu to rice and everything in between. You can also make the sauce to simply serve with your favorite other Indian dishes and even with some of the other options, like curry. To help make the recipe even healthier and more nutritious, you can use organic or all natural ingredients so that you do not need to worry about anything that is artificial.

# Chapter 7: Dinner Recipes

Dinners are a great way for you to be able to bring your family together. Most people eat dinner as one of the biggest meals of the day and things don't have to change just because you're a vegan. There are many vegan recipes for dinners that you can share with your friends, family, and other loved ones. They won't even know that you are feeding them something that will probably be the healthiest meal of the day.

**Dinner Recipe 1: Chili No Meat**

Level of Difficulty: 2

Preparation Time: 3 hours

Serving Size: 4

## You Will Need:

- 2 tin cans of kidney beans
- 1 tbsp of chili powder
- ½ of a glass jar of chili sauce
- 1 tin can of white beans
- ½ of a block of tofu
- 1 tsp of garlic
- 1 onion that is medium sized and white
- 1 bell pepper that is green

## Appliances Needed:

- Stove
- Stock Pot

## Directions

Start this recipe by cutting up your onion and your pepper and making sure that they are about the same size. This will help to make the chili easier for you to eat. Drain your beans and make sure that there is not a lot of liquid left in them. Add all of the ingredients to your stockpot and bring the mixture to a boil so that the ingredients get all incorporated together, and the flavor is the same throughout the rest of the dish. Once it has come to a boiling point, reduce your heat and let it simmer for 3 hours or until you are ready to eat it. Doing this will ensure that it is hot and thoroughly cooked. It will also help to further incorporate the flavors of the spices and can ensure that you are getting everything as tender as possible. The longer that you cook it, the more tender, it will be.

## Notes for this Recipe:

- Chili is your own thing. You can make this recipe any way that you like. Adding hot sauce or red pepper flakes to it will give it the familiar chili spice that you may be used to with non plant based food and adding other things to it can also increase the flavor. One tip that many people use for their chili is to put a small amount of liquid smoke in it. This will give it a smoky flavor that you would typically find in chili that has beef in it or has other meats that may have been smoked.

## Nutritional Information:

This is the nutritional information for one serving of the recipe.

| Calories | Fat | Sodium | Carbohydrates | Fiber | Sugar |
|---|---|---|---|---|---|
| 549 | 1.7 | 783 | 100 | 24 | 5 |

This recipe has all of the ingredients that you need for a meal that will really be able to stick to your ribs. This chili is a great option during the winter and will be able to leave you feeling full for the rest of the night. It is a recipe that families will be able to enjoy together. Consider making some type of side, like plant based biscuits, so that you will be able to have something to soak up the leftover chili with when you have finished eating the majority of it in the bowl.

# Dinner Recipe 2: Fauxghetti

Level of Difficulty: 2

Preparation Time: 1 hour

Serving Size: 4

## You Will Need:

- 1 large spaghetti squash
- 1 tin can of tomato paste
- 1 tin can of diced tomatoes
- 1 tsp of Italian seasoning
- 1 tsp of garlic powder
- 1 tin can of crushed tomatoes
- 1 tin can of tomato sauce

## Appliances Needed:

- Conventional oven
- Stove

## Directions

You must first start the recipe by cooking your spaghetti squash so that it comes apart into spaghetti "noodles" easily. Turn your oven on to 350 degrees and allow it to heat up. Once it is heated up, place the squash into the oven directly on the rack and allow it to cook for 20-30 minutes. It should be tender when you take it out of the oven. Once it has finished, take it out of the oven and make sure that it is adequately cooled off. Cut it from end to end and use a fork to pull the noodles out of it from the top to the bottom. Make sure that you have made a lot of noodles before you begin mixing it all together. While the spaghetti squash is in the oven, you can begin making your sauce. Combine all of your ingredients into a large pot on the stove. You may want to consider using a pot that is larger than what you need or even a stock pot so that you will be able to mix the squash in with the sauce once it has finished cooking. This will enable you to make sure that you have enough room to mix it up. Bring the sauce to a rolling boil and continue to stir until you are able to see that everything is mixing together. If you like your spaghetti sauce to be very smooth, use an immersion blender to mix it all together and blend it to the point where there are no big chunks left. Allow to simmer for around 10-15 minutes. Make sure that your sauce is warmed up and mix your squash in with it.

## Notes for this Recipe:

- Some people like to use onions and green peppers in their spaghetti sauce. You can make it in any way that you like but just make sure that you are ingredients that are in line with your plant based diet. If you plan to use onions and peppers to make your sauce, you will definitely want to make sure that you use an immersion blender so that you do not have large chunks of onions and peppers disrupting your spaghetti sauce.

## Nutritional Information:

This is the nutritional information for one serving of the recipe.

| Calories | Fat | Sodium | Carbohydrates | Fiber | Sugar |
|---|---|---|---|---|---|
| 113 | 0 | 139 | 6 | 12 | 4.3 |

While the recipe for this faux spaghetti will be able to satisfy any cravings that you have for traditional spaghetti, it is not quite as filling as some of the other recipes that are on the list. With only 113 calories per serving, you may want to consider serving this with another option on your dinner menu. You can make vegan garlic bread or any other side to go with this spaghetti. You can also up the serving size to help increase the nutritional value of each serving.

# Dinner Recipe 3: Skillet Mac

Level of Difficulty: 3

Preparation Time: 30 minutes

Serving Size: 4

## You Will Need:

- 1 package of vegan macaroni
- 1 small package of vegan beefless ground beef
- 1 tsp of olive oil
- ½ of a cup of onion
- 1 tsp of chili powder
- ½ of a tsp of cumin
- ½ of a tsp of paprika
- ½ of a cup of water
- 1 medium tomato
- 1 green onion

## Appliances Needed:

- Stove
- Skillet

## Directions

Begin your recipe by first cooking your pasta. Cook it on the stove until it is al dente. It should not be cooked more than that because the pasta will become too mushy when you start to cook it in the skillet. While the pasta is cooking, cut up all of your vegetables and make sure that they are about the same size as each other. Heat your olive oil up in your skillet and make sure that it is not boiling and that it does not get too hot. Add your vegetables so that they can start getting tender and the flavors can start getting combined. You can then add your water. Use the water from your pasta to add more flavor to the dish. Put the pasta into the skillet and cook on medium high heat or until the pasta and the vegetables are tender enough for you to be able to eat, and they will soften up. Do not overcook because the pasta will not be good if it has been cooked too much.

## Notes for this Recipe:

- Extra tomatoes in this recipe will give it extra flavor. You can also use garlic salt in place of the chili powder. There are many things that you can add to this to give it other flavors. You can also do different things that will make it taste different. There are some vegan cheese sauces that you can add to the recipe that will be able to make it cheesier.

## Nutritional Information:

This is the nutritional information for one serving of the recipe.

| Calories | Fat | Sodium | Carbohydrates | Fiber | Sugar |
|---|---|---|---|---|---|
| 222 | 1.5 | 9 | 2.3 | .8 | .8 |

There are many different factors that go into the nutritional value of this dish. It is a good idea to make sure that you are using the lowest calorie pasta possible. This will help to make the dish more nutritionally dense and will allow it to not take up too many calories while you are eating it for dinner. Make sure that you divide it into exactly 4 portions.

# Dinner Recipe 4: Tomatoes that are Stuffed

Level of Difficulty: 2

Preparation Time: 30 minutes

Serving Size: 4

## You Will Need:

- 6 tomatoes that have been hollowed out
- ¼ of a cup of olive oil
- 1 onion that is white
- 1 cup of quinoa that has been rinsed
- ¼ of a cup of pesto seasoning
- 1 bag of spinach
- ¼ of a tsp of garlic powder
- ½ of a tsp of Italian seasoning

## Appliances Needed:

- Stove
- Oven

## Directions

Chop your onion and cook it in a pan on your stove using the olive oil. Add the rest of the ingredients to the mixture and cook until the spinach has shrunk to a smaller amount. Make sure that it is all mixed up well and that you are able to combine it and mix it together. This is what will work as your filling so make sure that the quinoa, especially, is tender enough for you to be able to enjoy. Line your tomatoes up in a pan so that there are 3 on each side. Use a pan that is large enough for them to fit without getting smashed but make sure that it is small enough that they will not fall over or roll around in the pan. Set your oven to 400 degrees. Pack the tomatoes full of the filling and place them in the oven. Cook for 15-20 minutes or until the flesh of the tomatoes begins to get really tender and you can see that the filling is getting tender.

### Notes for this Recipe:

- For a more traditional route, you can use green peppers and cook the filling in the green peppers the same way that you would cook the tomatoes. This is also a recipe that you can freeze. Simply place the tomatoes in a disposable pan and do it the same way. Cover and mark with the date so that you know when you made them and when you can use them. If you want, you can add vegan cheese on top.

### Nutritional Information:

This is the nutritional information for one serving of the recipe.

| Calories | Fat | Sodium | Carbohydrates | Fiber | Sugar |
|---|---|---|---|---|---|
| 441 | 27.2 | 211 | 41.3 | 7.7 | 7.9 |

These stuffed tomatoes will give you a hot meal on a cold night or a quick recipe to make any time of the year. Each time that you make a batch to use right away consider making another batch to keep in the freezer. The nutritional information should stay the same no matter what you use since the nutritional value of the quinoa will be the same no matter what brand it is.

# Chapter 8: Dessert Recipes

Just because you're trying to live a healthier lifestyle does not mean that you need to swear off all desserts. These desserts are all plant based and will be able to help you stick to the eating patterns that you are trying to do with your vegan diet. The recipes for these desserts are going to be able to suit your needs no matter what. Make them as a sweet treat for after dinner or just something fun any time of the day.

# Dessert Recipe 1: Apple Pie

Level of Difficulty: 3

Preparation Time: 1 hour

Serving Size: 8

## You Will Need:

- 1 cup of brown sugar that is light
- ¼ of a cup of coconut milk
- 1 cup of dairy free butter, divided
- 1 tsp of vanilla extract
- 2 ½ of a cup of white flour
- ¼ of a cup of powdered sug
- 1/3 of a cup of cold water
- 6 large apples
- 2 tsp of cinnamon
- 1 tsp of apple pie spice
- 1 tbsp of corn starch

## Appliances Needed:

- Stove
- Oven

## Directions

Combine all of the ingredients except for half of the butter and the flour into a pot and put on the stove over medium heat. Heat it up until it is just before boiling and make sure that all of the apples are chopped up into small pieces so that they will fit nicely into the pie. While this is cooking, make your dough by mixing the flour, the butter, and the cold water. You can then divide the dough into a bottom piece and a top piece. Put the bottom piece into your pie pan. Fill the pan (and the dough) with the apple pie filling that you just made on the stove and top with the other piece of dough. You can cut and weave for a traditional apple pie look. You can also just poke holes in the top of it to make sure that the steam from the apples is able to escape. Heat your oven to 350 degrees and cook for 35 minutes. The crust should be golden brown.

## Notes for this Recipe:

- If you want to take a shortcut on the recipe, look for an apple pie filling that is already made that does not have any animal byproducts in it. This can be difficult, but you may want to check at one of your local natural food stores or even order it online. No matter what type of filling you use, this is the recipe that you should use for the crust so that it is dairy and animal free.

## Nutritional Information:

This is the nutritional information for one serving of the recipe.

| Calories | Fat | Sodium | Carbohydrates | Fiber | Sugar |
|----------|-----|--------|---------------|-------|-------|
| 343      | 2   | 27     | 37.7          | 3.9   | 27.3  |

There is a lot of sugar in this recipe. It is intended to be a dessert recipe and should be treated as such. This is not a good recipe to eat everyday, and you should try to save it for when you simply need a sweet treat. While it is plant based, does not necessarily mean that it is completely healthy for you to consume it every day.

# Dessert Recipe 2: Strawberry Ice No Cream

Level of Difficulty: 1

Preparation Time: 5 hours

Serving Size: 4

## You Will Need:

- Strawberries, 2 cups that have been frozen
- 1 full tin can of coconut milk
- ½ of a cup of sugar or natural sweetener
- ½ of a teasp of vanilla extract

## Appliances Needed:

- Food processor
- Freezer

## Directions

Make sure that your strawberries are small enough to fit in your food processor and that they are going to blend well. They do not have to be frozen, but it will be easier for you to be able to make sure that they are blended properly. You can easily freeze fresh strawberries by popping them into the freezer for a few hours before you decide to make your ice cream. Place the rest of the ingredients into your food processor and blend until it is smooth and creamy. Stir it a few times to mix up the sides with the rest of the ingredients and blend it again so that you can be sure that it is fully mixed up. When it is done, scrape it into a small bread pan and cover it with plastic wrap. Place it in the freezer and let it get frozen for, at least, 5 hours. If you leave it longer, the ice cream will be firmer and more like traditional ice cream. The shorter period of time that you leave it in the freezer, the easier it will be to scoop it out.

## Notes for this Recipe:

- This recipe is for strawberry, but you can use any fruit that you would like to make it different flavors of ice cream. You can even use an extra can of coconut milk or something similar to make ice cream that is strictly vanilla flavored. Don't be afraid to experiment with the different ways to make the ice cream and the different things that you can add into it. Just make sure that whatever you add to it is vegan and completely plant based to help you maintain your healthy lifestyle.

## Nutritional Information:

This is the nutritional information for one serving of the recipe.

| Calories | Fat | Sodium | Carbohydrates | Fiber | Sugar |
|---|---|---|---|---|---|
| 340 | 22.3 | 18 | 37.1 | 3.5 | 30.2 |

Different fruit may have different nutritional information. Take this into consideration before you rely on the nutritional information. If you make the recipe as it was intended to be, you will be able to be sure that the nutritional information is accurate. Most commercial coconut milk and sugar have the same nutrients in them, so that will make it much easier for you when you are counting the nutrients in it.

# Dessert Recipe 3: Brownies Minus the Guilt

Level of Difficulty: 3

Preparation Time: 1 hour

Serving Size: 16

## You Will Need:

- ¼ of a cup of peanut butter
- ½ of a cup of brown sugar
- 1/3 of a cup of maple syrup
- ¼ of a cup of coconut oil that has been melted
- ½ of a cup of dark chocolate chips
- ¼ of a cup of flour
- 2 tbsp ground flax seed
- ¼ cup of water
- 1/2 of a tsp of salt
- 1 tsp of vanilla
- ¾ of a cup of cocoa powder

## Appliances Needed:

- Oven

## Directions

Start by mixing all of your wet ingredients together in a bowl. In a separate bowl, mix all of your dry ingredients together. Set your oven to 325 degrees and prepare a square pan with coconut oil rubbed on the inside of it. Once you have mixed up your dry ingredients and your wet ingredients, add them together and stir to make sure that they are thoroughly incorporated with each other. Make sure that there are no clumps aside from the chocolate chips that you put in there. You should also make sure that the coconut oil is melted the whole way before you put it into the recipe. This will ensure that it does not get as clumpy and that the mixture is as smooth as possible. Place the mixture into your pan that you already coated with coconut oil and place it in the preheated oven. Cook for around 30-40 minutes. The brownies are done when you take them out and a toothpick inserted into the center of them comes out clean instead of with liquid or crumbles on it. Make sure that they have time to cool off for, at least, one hour before you decide to serve them.

## Notes for this Recipe:

- These brownies are great on their own, or they make a great base for different types of brownies. For a festive Christmas brownie, add peppermint extract and chopped peppermints to the mixture. For a milder peanut butter taste, swap out the peanut butter for almond butter before you start the recipe. If you want them to have more of a peanut flavor to them, you can also add chopped peanuts to the mixture and on the top of the brownies so that you will be able to have a little bit of crunch when you are eating the brownies. You can add anything to this batter or the top of these brownies to help change up the flavor.

## Nutritional Information:

This is the nutritional information for one serving of the recipe.

| Calories | Fat | Sodium | Carbohydrates | Fiber | Sugar |
|---|---|---|---|---|---|
| 361 | 36 | 236 | 34.8 | 6.8 | 24 |

Just like traditional brownies, these may not be your best option for every day. They do make a nice treat, though, and you can enjoy them without feeling bad about busting your plant based diet. This is something that you can use as an after dinner treat or simply when you need to have a sweet snack throughout the day. When you add different ingredients to the brownie batter or on top, it will change the nutritional information of the brownies.

# Conclusion

Thank for making it through to the end of this book, let's hope it was informative and able to provide you with all of the tools you need to achieve your goals whatever they may be.

Finally, if you found this book useful in anyway, a review on Amazon is always appreciated!

Made in the USA
Lexington, KY
08 March 2017